To Irvin & Chris

May God bless you in Yeshua
our Lord

Keith

THE GOOD NEWS OF
YESHUA THE MESSIAH,
AS REPORTED BY

YOCHANAN

(JOHN)

THE GOOD NEWS OF
YESHUA THE MESSIAH,
AS REPORTED BY

YOCHANAN

(JOHN)

From the
Jewish New Testament

by

David H. Stern

"...salvation comes from the Jews."
— Yochanan 4:22

JEWISH NEW TESTAMENT PUBLICATIONS
Post Office Box 1313, Clarksville, Maryland 21029, U.S.A.
Israel office: 78 Manahat, 96901, Jerusalem, Israel

Published by
JEWISH NEW TESTAMENT PUBLICATIONS
Post Office Box 1313, Clarksville, Maryland 21029 U.S.A.
Write or call 301/764-6144 for quantity discounts.

Israel office: 78 Manahat, 96901, Jerusalem, Israel

First Edition

Cover illustration by Mickey Klugman
Typeset in Times Roman
by Barry Segal International, Jerusalem, Israel

Printed in the United States of America
ISBN 965–359–004–9

INTRODUCTION

I. WHY *YOCHANAN?*

The Good News of Yeshua the Messiah, as Reported by Yochanan (John) presents Yeshua from Natzeret (Jesus of Nazareth) as both Messiah of Israel and Son of God. In this selection from the *Jewish New Testament,* Christians can perceive that the Messianic Community (the Church) has not replaced the Jews as God's people, and that their own faith is far more Jewish than they may have thought. Jews, in turn, can see that neither Yeshua nor John's Gospel is antisemitic, as is sometimes charged.

In fact it is precisely because of *Yochanan's* undeserved antisemitic reputation that it has been chosen to be the first separately published *Jewish New Testament* excerpt. Most versions of John sound vehemently critical of "the Jews." But the correct rendering of the Greek word often translated "Jews" should be the more specific word "Judeans."

In first century Israel, those who believed in Yeshua were Jews. They were just as Jewish as the Jews who did not believe in him. It would have made no sense for the New Testament writers to inveigh indiscriminately against *all* Jews. Rather, the specific reference bespeaks the rivalry which existed between the more religiously strict Judeans and the simpler country folk of the Galil, home of Yeshua and his *talmidim* (disciples). The rendering in *Yochanan* reflects this rivalry and at the same time removes the antisemitism stigma.

Futhermore, the reader will discover that *Yochanan* is a very Jewish gospel indeed. Consider the first and fourteenth verses of Chapter 1. On the surface they seem to convey a very *un*-Jewish idea, namely that the *man* Yeshua had divine origins:

> *In the beginning was the Word, and the Word was with God, and the Word was God....The Word became a human being and lived with us, and we saw his* Sh'khinah [Hebrew for "God's manifest glory"], *the* Sh'khinah *of the Father's only Son, full of grace and truth.*

It is a common misconception that Yeshua, a man, decided he was God — or that Sha'ul (Paul) decided that for him. *Yochanan* presents the opposite picture: the Word who "was God" actually "became a human being" and shared human fate. The New Testament, expanding on material from the *Tanakh* (Old Testament) such as Isaiah 52:13–53:12, explains that Yeshua did this for our sakes in order to save us from a terrible end from which we could not save ourselves.

Moreover, the very idea of "the Word" is also Jewish in origin. Although the Greek word for "Word" is *logos*, and pagan Greek religion considered the *logos* to be a high spiritual entity, Judaism had a concept called *memra* (Aramaic for "word"). The *memra* had both divine and human characteristics. "In the beginning was the *memra*...and the *memra* was God" expresses this Jewish truth.

Conventional wisdom decrees that Christianity is Christianity and Judaism is Judaism and never the twain shall meet. In other words, the common view is that although first-century Judaism was the crucible in which Christianity was forged, the latter quickly moved away from Judaism and became a religion incompatible with it. But those of us who are Messianic Jews, Jews who follow Yeshua and adhere to his teaching, are living testimony to the impossibility of keeping New Testament faith forever separated from Judaism. Messianic Jews are 100% Jewish and 100% Messianic. The task of bringing the New Testament back into a Jewish framework is essential if Jews and Christians are to bridge 2,000 years of misunderstanding. *The Good News of Yeshua the Messiah, as Reported by Yochanan (John)* helps accomplish this goal.

II. ABOUT THE *JEWISH NEW TESTAMENT*

The *Jewish New Testament* translation differs from other versions because it uniquely expresses the New Testament's original and essential Jewishness. It does so in three ways:
- Cosmetically — by using neutral terms and Hebrew names, such as "execution stake" instead of "cross," "Ya'akov" instead of "James."
- Culturally and religiously — by highlighting Jewish features such as "Chanukkah" not "the feast of dedication" *(Yochanan 10:22), "Torah"* instead of "law."
- Theologically — by correcting mistranslations resulting from anti-Jewish theological bias, the best example in *Yochanan* being "the Judeans" instead of "the Jews," as previously explained.

Freshly rendered from the original Greek into enjoyable modern English, the *Jewish New Testament* challenges Jews to understand that Yeshua is a friend to every Jewish heart and the New Testament a Jewish book filled with truths to be accepted and acted upon. At the same time, while reaffirming the equality of Gentiles and Jews in the Messianic Community, it challenges Christians to acknowledge not only the Jewishness of their faith but their oneness with the Jewish people.

If Christians come to experience their oneness with the Jewish people and Jews come to trust in Yeshua the Messiah, this publication will be doing its work.

THE GOOD NEWS OF YESHUA THE MESSIAH,
AS REPORTED BY

YOCHANAN (JOHN)

¹ In the beginning was the Word,
and the Word was with God,

And the Word was God.

² He was with God in the beginning.

³ All things came to be through him,
and without him nothing made had
being.

⁴ In him was life,
and the life was the light of mankind.

⁵ The light shines in the darkness,
and the darkness has not suppressed
it.

⁶ There was a man sent from God
whose name was Yochanan. ⁷ He came
to be a testimony, to bear witness
concerning the light; so that through
him, everyone might put his trust in
God and be faithful to him. ⁸ He himself
was not that light; no, he came to bear
witness concerning the light.

⁹ This was the true light,
which gives light to everyone entering
the world.

¹⁰ He was in the world — the world
came to be through him —
yet the world did not know him.

¹¹ He came to his own homeland,
yet his own people did not receive
him.

¹² But to as many as did receive him, to
those who put their trust in his person
and power, he gave the right to become
children of God, ¹³ not because of
bloodline, physical impulse or human
intention, but because of God.

¹⁴ The Word became a human being
and lived with us,
and we saw his *Sh'khinah*,

The *Sh'khinah* of the Father's only
Son,
full of grace and truth.

¹⁵ Yochanan witnessed concerning
him when he cried out, "This is the man
I was talking about when I said, 'The
one coming after me has come to rank
ahead of me, because he existed before
me.'"

¹⁶ We have all received from his fullness,
yes, grace upon grace.

¹⁷ For the *Torah* was given through
Moshe;
grace and truth came through Yeshua
the Messiah.

¹⁸ No one has ever seen God; but the
only and unique Son, who is identical
with God and is at the Father's side —
he has made him known.

¹⁹ Here is Yochanan's testimony:
when the Judeans sent *cohanim* and
L'viim from Yerushalayim to ask him,
"Who are you?" ²⁰ he was very straight-
forward and stated clearly, "I am not
the Messiah." ²¹ "Then who are you?"
they asked him. "Are you Eliyahu?"
"No, I am not," he said. "Are you 'the

prophet', the one we're expecting?" "No," he replied. ²² So they said to him, "Who are you? — so that we can give an answer to the people who sent us. What do you have to say about yourself?" ²³ He answered in the words of Yesha'yahu the prophet, "I am

The voice of someone crying out: 'In the desert make the way of *Adonai* straight!'"ᵃ

²⁴ Some of those who had been sent were *P'rushim*. ²⁵ They asked him, "If you are neither the Messiah nor Eliyahu nor 'the prophet', then why are you immersing people?" ²⁶ To them Yochanan replied, "I am immersing people in water, but among you is standing someone whom you don't know. ²⁷ He is the one coming after me — I'm not good enough even to untie his sandal!" ²⁸ All this took place in Beit-Anyah, east of the Yarden, where Yochanan was immersing.

²⁹ The next day, Yochanan saw Yeshua coming toward him and said, "Look! God's lamb! The one who is taking away the sin of the world! ³⁰ This is the man I was talking about when I said, 'After me is coming someone who has come to rank above me, because he existed before me.' ³¹ I myself did not know who he was, but the reason I came immersing with water was so that he might be made known to Israel." ³² Then Yochanan gave this testimony: "I saw the Spirit coming down from heaven like a dove, and remaining on him. ³³ I myself did not know who he was, but the one who sent me to immerse in water said to me, 'The one on whom you see the Spirit descending and remaining, this is the one who immerses in the *Ruach HaKodesh*.'

³⁴ And I have seen and borne witness that this is the Son of God."

³⁵ The next day, Yochanan was again standing with two of his *talmidim*. ³⁶ On seeing Yeshua walking by, he said, "Look! God's lamb!" ³⁷ His two *talmidim* heard him speaking, and they followed Yeshua. ³⁸ Yeshua turned and saw them following him, and he asked them, "What are you looking for?" They said to him, "Rabbi!" (which means "Teacher!") "Where are you staying?" ³⁹ He said to them, "Come and see." So they went and saw where he was staying, and remained with him the rest of the day — it was about four o'clock in the afternoon. ⁴⁰ One of the two who had heard Yochanan and had followed Yeshua was Andrew the brother of Shim'on Kefa. ⁴¹ The first thing he did was to find his brother Shim'on and tell him, "We've found the *Mashiach*!" (The word means "one who has been anointed".) ⁴² He took him to Yeshua. Looking at him, Yeshua said, "You are Shim'on Bar-Yochanan;

A·do·nai — the LORD, Jehovah
Beit-An·yah — Bethany
co·ha·nim — priests
E·li·ya·hu — Elijah
L'vi·im — Levites
Ma·shi·ach — Messiah
Mo·she — Moses
P'ru·shim — Pharisees
Ru·ach-Ha·Ko·desh — Holy Spirit
Shim·'on — Simon
Shim·'on Bar-Yo·cha·nan — Simon, son of John
Shim·'on Ke·fa — Simon Peter
Sh'khi·nah — God's manifest glory
tal·mi·dim — disciples
To·rah — Teaching, "Law"; Pentateuch
Yar·den — Jordan
Ye·ru·sha·la·yim — Jerusalem
Ye·sha'·ya·hu — Isaiah
Ye·shu·a — Jesus
Yo·cha·nan — John

ᵃ Isaiah 40:3

you will be known as Kefa." (The name means "rock".)

⁴³ The next day, having decided to leave for the Galil, Yeshua found Philip and said, "Follow me!" ⁴⁴ Philip was from Beit-Tzaidah, the town where Andrew and Kefa lived. ⁴⁵ Philip found Natan'el and told him, "We've found the one that Moshe wrote about in the *Torah*, also the Prophets — it's Yeshua Ben-Yosef from Natzeret!" ⁴⁶ Natan'el answered him, "Natzeret? Can anything good come from there?" "Come and see," Philip said to him. ⁴⁷ Yeshua saw Natan'el coming toward him and remarked about him, "Here's a true son of Israel — nothing false in him!" ⁴⁸ Natan'el said to him, "How do you know me?" Yeshua answered him, "Before Philip called you, when you were under the fig tree, I saw you." ⁴⁹ Natan'el said, "Rabbi, you are the Son of God! You are the King of Israel!" ⁵⁰ Yeshua answered him, "You believe all this just because I told you I saw you under the fig tree? You will see greater things than that!" ⁵¹ Then he said to him, "Yes indeed! I tell you that you will see **heaven** opened and **the angels of God going up and coming down**^{b} on the Son of Man!"

2 ¹ Two days later, there was a wedding at Kanah in the Galil; and the mother of Yeshua was there. ² Yeshua too was invited to the wedding, along with his *talmidim*. ³ The wine ran out, and Yeshua's mother said to him, "They have no more wine." ⁴ Yeshua replied, "Mother, why should that concern me? — or you? My time hasn't come yet." ⁵ His mother said to the servants, "Do whatever he tells you." ⁶ Now six stone water-jars were standing there for the Jewish ceremonial washings, each with a capacity of twenty or thirty gallons. ⁷ Yeshua told them, "Fill the jars with water," and they filled them to the brim. ⁸ He said, "Now draw some out, and take it to the man in charge of the banquet;" and they took it. ⁹ The man in charge tasted the water; it had now turned into wine! He did not know where it had come from, but the servants who had drawn the water knew. So he called the bridegroom ¹⁰ and said to him, "Everyone else serves the good wine first and the poorer wine after people have drunk freely. But you have kept the good wine until now!" ¹¹ This, the first of Yeshua's miraculous signs, he did at Kanah in the Galil; he manifested his glory, and his *talmidim* came to trust in him. ¹² Afterwards, he, his mother and brothers, and his *talmidim* went down to K'far-Nachum and stayed there a few days.

¹³ It was almost time for the festival of *Pesach* in Y'hudah, so Yeshua went up to Yerushalayim. ¹⁴ In the Temple grounds he found those who were selling cattle, sheep and pigeons, and others who were sitting at tables exchanging money. ¹⁵ He made a whip from cords and drove them all out of the Temple grounds, the sheep and cattle as well. He knocked over the money-changers' tables, scattering their coins; ¹⁶ and to the pigeon-sellers he said, "Get these things out of here! How dare you turn my Father's house into a market?" ¹⁷ (His *talmidim* later recalled that the *Tanakh* says, **"Zeal for your house will devour me."**)^c ¹⁸ So the Judeans confronted him by asking him, "What miraculous sign can you show us to prove you have the right to do all this?" ¹⁹ Yeshua answered them, "Destroy this temple, and in three days I will raise it up again." ²⁰ The Judeans said,

---

b Genesis 28:12

c Psalm 69:10(9)

"It took 46 years to build this Temple, and you're going to raise it in three days?" ²¹But the "temple" he had spoken of was his body. ²²Therefore, when he was raised from the dead, his *talmidim* remembered that he had said this, and they trusted in the *Tanakh* and in what Yeshua had said.

²³Now while Yeshua was in Yerushalayim at the *Pesach* festival, there were many people who "believed in his name" when they saw the miracles he performed. ²⁴But he did not commit himself to them, for he knew what people are like — ²⁵that is, he didn't need anyone to inform him about a person, because he knew what was in the person's heart.

3 ¹There was a man among the *P'rushim*, named Nakdimon, who was a ruler of the Judeans. ²This man came to Yeshua by night and said to him, "Rabbi, we know it is from God that you have come as a teacher; for no one can do these miracles you perform unless God is with him." ³"Yes, indeed," Yeshua answered him, "I tell you that unless a person is born again from above, he cannot see the Kingdom of God."

⁴Nakdimon said to him, "How can a grown man be 'born'? Can he go back into his mother's womb and be born a second time?" ⁵Yeshua answered, "Yes, indeed, I tell you that unless a person is born from water and the Spirit, he cannot enter the Kingdom of God. ⁶What is born from the flesh is flesh, and what is born from the Spirit is spirit. ⁷Stop being amazed at my telling you that you must be born again from above! ⁸The wind blows where it wants to, and you hear its sound, but you don't know where it comes from or where it's going. That's how it is with everyone who has been born from the Spirit."

⁹Nakdimon replied, "How can this happen?" ¹⁰Yeshua answered him, "You hold the office of teacher in Israel, and you don't know this? ¹¹Yes, indeed! I tell you that what we speak about, we know; and what we give evidence of, we have seen; but you people don't accept our evidence! ¹²If you people don't believe me when I tell you about the things of the world, how will you believe me when I tell you about the things of heaven? ¹³No one has gone up into heaven; there is only the one who has come down from heaven, the Son of Man. ¹⁴Just as Moshe lifted up the serpent in the desert, so must the Son of Man be lifted up; ¹⁵so that everyone who trusts in him may have eternal life.

¹⁶"For God so loved the world that he gave his only and unique Son, so that everyone who trusts in him may have eternal life, instead of being utterly destroyed. ¹⁷For God did not send the Son into the world to judge the world, but rather so that through him, the world might be saved. ¹⁸Those who trust in him are not judged; those who do not trust have been judged already,

---

Beit-Tzai·**dah** — Bethsaida
the Ga·**lil** — Galilee
Ka·**nah** — Cana
Ke·**fa** — Peter
K'far-Na·**chum** — Capernaum
Mo·**she** — Moses
Nak·di·**mon** — Nicodemus
Na·tan·'**el** — Nathanael
Na·tze·ret — Nazareth
Pe·sach — Passover
P'ru·shim — Pharisees
tal·mi·dim — disciples
Ta·nakh — Hebrew Scriptures, "Old Testament"
To·rah — Teaching, "Law"; Pentateuch
Ye·ru·sha·la·yim — Jerusalem
Ye·shu·a — Jesus
Ye·shu·a Ben-Yo·sef — Jesus, son of Joseph
Y'hu·dah — Judea

in that they have not trusted in the one who is God's only and unique Son.
¹⁹ "Now this is the judgment: the light has come into the world, but people loved the darkness rather than the light. Why? Because their actions were wicked. ²⁰ For everyone who does evil things hates the light and avoids it, so that his actions won't be exposed. ²¹ But everyone who does what is true comes to the light, so that all may see that his actions are accomplished through God."

²² After this, Yeshua and his *talmidim* went out into the countryside of Y'hudah, where he stayed awhile with them and immersed people. ²³ Yochanan too was immersing at Einayim, near Shalem, because there was plenty of water there; and people kept coming to be immersed. ²⁴ (This was before Yochanan's imprisonment.)

²⁵ A discussion arose between some of Yochanan's *talmidim* and a Judean about ceremonial washing; ²⁶ and they came to Yochanan and said to him, "Rabbi, you know the man who was with you on the other side of the Yarden, the one you spoke about? Well, here he is, immersing; and everyone is going to him!" ²⁷ Yochanan answered, "No one can receive anything unless it has been given to him from Heaven. ²⁸ You yourselves can confirm that I did not say I was the Messiah, but that I have been sent ahead of him. ²⁹ The bridegroom is the one who has the bride; but the bridegroom's friend, who stands and listens to him, is overjoyed at the sound of the bridegroom's voice. So this joy of mine is now complete. ³⁰ He must become more important, while I become less important.

³¹ "He who comes from above is above all. He who is from the earth is from the earth and talks from an earthly point of view; he who comes from heaven is above all. ³² He testifies about what he has actually seen and heard, yet no one accepts what he says! ³³ Whoever does accept what he says puts his seal on the fact that God is true, ³⁴ because the one whom God sent speaks God's words. For God does not give him the Spirit in limited degree — ³⁵ the Father loves the Son and has put everything in his hands. ³⁶ Whoever trusts in the Son has eternal life. But whoever disobeys the Son will not see that life but remains subject to God's wrath."

4 ¹ When Yeshua learned that the P'rushim had heard he was making and immersing more *talmidim* than Yochanan ² (although it was not Yeshua himself who immersed but his *talmidim*), ³ Yeshua left Y'hudah and set out again for the Galil. ⁴ This meant that he had to pass through Shomron.

⁵ He came to a town in Shomron called Sh'khem, near the field Ya'akov had given to his son Yosef. ⁶ Ya'akov's Well was there; so Yeshua, exhausted from his travel, sat down by the well; it was about noon. ⁷ A woman from Shomron came to draw some water; and Yeshua said to her, "Give me a drink of water." ⁸ (His *talmidim* had gone into town to buy food.) ⁹ The woman from Shomron said to him, "How is it that you, a Jew, ask for water from me, a woman of Shomron?" (For Jews don't associate with people from Shomron.) ¹⁰ Yeshua answered her, "If you knew God's gift, that is, who it is saying to you, 'Give me a drink of water,' then you would have asked him; and he would have given you living water."

¹¹ She said to him, "Sir, you don't have a bucket, and the well is deep; so where do you get this 'living water'? ¹² You aren't greater than our father

Ya'akov, are you? He gave us this well and drank from it, and so did his sons and his cattle." ¹³Yeshua answered, "Everyone who drinks this water will get thirsty again, ¹⁴but whoever drinks the water I will give him will never be thirsty again! On the contrary, the water I give him will become a spring of water inside him, welling up into eternal life!"

¹⁵"Sir, give me this water," the woman said to him, "so that I won't have to be thirsty and keep coming here to draw water." ¹⁶He said to her, "Go, call your husband, and come back." ¹⁷She answered, "I don't have a husband." Yeshua said to her, "You're right, you don't have a husband! ¹⁸You've had five husbands in the past, and you're not married to the man you're living with now! You've spoken the truth!"

¹⁹"Sir, I can see that you are a prophet," the woman replied. ²⁰"Our fathers worshipped on this mountain, but you people say that the place where one has to worship is in Yerushalayim." ²¹Yeshua said, "Lady, believe me, the time is coming when you will worship the Father neither on this mountain nor in Yerushalayim. ²²You people don't know what you are worshipping; we worship what we do know, because salvation comes from the Jews. ²³But the time is coming — indeed, it's here now — when the true worshippers will worship the Father spiritually and truly, for these are the kind of people the Father wants worshipping him. ²⁴God is spirit; and worshippers must worship him spiritually and truly."

²⁵The woman replied, "I know that *Mashiach* is coming" (that is, "the one who has been anointed"). "When he comes, he will tell us everything." ²⁶Yeshua said to her, "I, the person speaking to you, am he."

²⁷Just then, his *talmidim* arrived.

They were amazed that he was talking with a woman; but none of them said, "What do you want?" or, "Why are you talking with her?" ²⁸So the woman left her water-jar, went back to the town and said to the people there, ²⁹"Come, see a man who told me everything I've ever done. Could it be that this is the Messiah?" ³⁰They left the town and began coming toward him.

³¹Meanwhile, the *talmidim* were urging Yeshua, "Rabbi, eat something." ³²But he answered, "I have food to eat that you don't know about." ³³At this, the *talmidim* asked one another, "Could someone have brought him food?" ³⁴Yeshua said to them, "My food is to do what the one who sent me wants and to bring his work to completion. ³⁵Don't you have a saying, 'Four more months and then the harvest'? Well, what I say to you is: open your eyes and look at the fields! They're already ripe for harvest! ³⁶The one who reaps receives his wages and gathers fruit for eternal life, so that the reaper and the sower may be glad together — ³⁷for in this matter, the proverb, 'One sows and another reaps,' holds true. ³⁸I sent you to reap what you haven't worked for. Others have done the hard labor, and you have benefitted from their work."

Ei·**na**·yim — Aenon, Enon
the Ga·**lil** — Galilee
Ma·shi·ach — Messiah
P'ru·shim — Pharisees
Sha·lem — Salim
Sh'**khem** — Sychar
Shom·ron — Samaria
tal·mi·dim — disciples
Ya·'a·**kov** — Jacob
Yar·den — Jordan
Ye·ru·sha·**la**·yim — Jerusalem
Ye·**shu**·a — Jesus
Y'hu·**dah** — Judea
Yo·cha·**nan** — John
Yo·**sef** — Joseph

³⁹ Many people from that town in Shomron put their trust in him because of the woman's testimony, "He told me all the things I did." ⁴⁰ So when these people from Shomron came to him, they asked him to stay with them. He stayed two days, ⁴¹ and many more came to trust because of what he said. ⁴² They said to the woman, "We no longer trust because of what you said, because we have heard for ourselves. We know indeed that this man really is the Savior of the world."

⁴³ After the two days, he went on from there toward the Galil. ⁴⁴ Now Yeshua himself said, "A prophet is not respected in his own country." ⁴⁵ But when he arrived in the Galil, the people there welcomed him, because they had seen all he had done at the festival in Yerushalayim; since they had been there too.

⁴⁶ He went again to Kanah in the Galil, where he had turned the water into wine. An officer in the royal service was there; his son was ill in K'far-Nachum. ⁴⁷ This man, on hearing that Yeshua had come from Y'hudah to the Galil, went and asked him to come down and heal his son, for he was at the point of death. ⁴⁸ Yeshua answered, "Unless you people see signs and miracles, you simply will not trust!" ⁴⁹ The officer said to him, "Sir, come down before my child dies." ⁵⁰ Yeshua replied, "You may go, your son is alive." The man believed what Yeshua said and left. ⁵¹ As he was going down, his servants met him with the news that his son was alive. ⁵² So he asked them at what time he had gotten better; and they said, "The fever left him yesterday at one o'clock in the afternoon." ⁵³ The father knew that that was the very hour when Yeshua had told him, "Your son is alive;" and he and all his household trusted. ⁵⁴ This was a second sign that Yeshua did; he

did it after he had come from Y'hudah into the Galil.

5 ¹ After this, there was a Judean festival; and Yeshua went up to Yerushalayim. ² In Yerushalayim, by the Sheep Gate, is a pool called in Aramaic, Beit-Zata, ³ in which lay a crowd of invalids — blind, lame, crippled. ⁴* ⁵ One man was there who had been ill for 38 years. ⁶ Yeshua, seeing this man and knowing that he had been there a long time, said to him, "Do you want to be healed?" ⁷ The sick man answered, "I have no one to put me in the pool when the water is disturbed; and while I'm trying to get there, someone goes in ahead of me." ⁸ Yeshua said to him, "Get up, pick up your mat and walk!" ⁹ Immediately the man was healed, and he picked up his mat and walked.

Now that day was *Shabbat*, ¹⁰ so the Judeans said to the man who had been healed, "It's *Shabbat*! It's against *Torah* for you to carry your mat!" ¹¹ But he answered them, "The man who healed me — he's the one who told me, 'Pick up your mat and walk.'" ¹² They asked him, "Who is the man who told you to pick it up and walk?" ¹³ But the man who had been healed didn't know who it was, because Yeshua had slipped away into the crowd.

¹⁴ Afterwards Yeshua found him in the Temple court and said to him, "See, you are well! Now stop sinning, or something worse may happen to you!" ¹⁵ The man went off and told the Judeans it was Yeshua who had healed

---

* Some manuscripts have verses 3b-4:..., waiting for the water to move; ⁴ for at certain times an angel of *Adonai* went down into the pool and disturbed the water, and whoever stepped into the water first after it was disturbed was healed of whatever disease he had.

7

him; 16 and on account of this, the Judeans began harassing Yeshua because he did these things on *Shabbat*. 17 But he answered them, "My Father has been working until now, and I too am working." 18 This answer made the Judeans all the more intent on killing him — not only was he breaking *Shabbat*; but also, by saying that God was his own Father, he was claiming equality with God. 19 Therefore, Yeshua said this to them: "Yes, indeed! I tell you that the Son cannot do anything on his own, but only what he sees the Father doing; whatever the Father does, the Son does too. 20 For the Father loves the Son and shows him everything he does; and he will show him even greater things than these, so that you will be amazed. 21 Just as the Father raises the dead and makes them alive, so too the Son makes alive anyone he wants. 22 The Father does not judge anyone but has entrusted all judgment to the Son, 23 so that all may honor the Son as they honor the Father. Whoever fails to honor the Son is not honoring the Father who sent him. 24 Yes, indeed! I tell you that whoever hears what I am saying and trusts the one who sent me has eternal life — that is, he will not come up for judgment but has already crossed over from death to life! 25 Yes, indeed! I tell you that there is coming a time — in fact, it's already here — when the dead will hear the voice of the Son of God, and those who listen will come to life. 26 For just as the Father has life in himself, so he has given the Son life to have in himself. 27 Also he has given him authority to execute judgment, because he is the Son of Man. 28 Don't be surprised at this; because the time is coming when all who are in the grave will hear his voice 29 and come out — those who have done good to a resurrection of

life, and those who have done evil to a resurrection of judgment. 30 I can't do a thing on my own. As I hear, I judge; and my judgment is right; because I don't seek my own desire, but the desire of the one who sent me.

31 "If I testify on my own behalf, my testimony is not valid. 32 But there is someone else testifying on my behalf, and I know that the testimony he is making is valid — 33 you have sent to Yochanan, and he has testified to the truth. 34 Not that I collect human testimony; rather, I say these things so that you might be saved. 35 He was a lamp burning and shining, and for a little while you were willing to bask in his light.

36 "But I have a testimony that is greater than Yochanan's. For the things the Father has given me to do, the very things I am doing now, testify on my behalf that the Father has sent me.

37 "In addition, the Father who sent me has himself testified on my behalf. But you have never heard his voice or seen his shape; 38 moreover, his word does not stay in you, because you don't trust the one he sent. 39 You keep examining the *Tanakh* because you think that in it you have eternal life. Those very Scriptures bear witness to me,

---

A·do·**nai** — the LORD, Jehovah
Beit-Za·ta — Bethzatha
the Ga·**lil** — Galilee
Ka·**nah** — Cana
K'far-Na·**chum** — Capernaum
Shab·bat — the Sabbath
Shom·ron — Samaria
Ta·nakh — Hebrew Scriptures, "Old Testament"
To·rah — Teaching, "Law"; Pentateuch
Ye·ru·sha·**la**·yim — Jerusalem
Ye·**shu**·a — Jesus
Y'hu·**dah** — Judea
Yo·cha·**nan** — John

⁴⁰ but you won't come to me in order to have life! ⁴¹ "I don't collect praise from men, ⁴² but I do know you people — I know that you have no love for God in you! ⁴³ I have come in my Father's name, and you don't accept me; if someone else comes in his own name, him you will accept. ⁴⁴ How can you trust? You're busy collecting praise from each other, instead of seeking praise from God only.

⁴⁵ "But don't think that it is I who will be your accuser before the Father. Do you know who will accuse you? Moshe, the very one you have counted on! ⁴⁶ For if you really believed Moshe, you would believe me; because it was about me that he wrote. ⁴⁷ But if you don't believe what he wrote, how are you going to believe what I say?"

6 ¹ Some time later, Yeshua went over to the far side of Lake Kinneret (that is, Lake Tiberias), ² and a large crowd followed him, because they had seen the miracles he had performed on the sick. ³ Yeshua went up into the hills and sat down there with his *talmidim*. ⁴ Now the Judean festival of *Pesach* was coming up; ⁵ so when Yeshua looked up and saw that a large crowd was approaching, he said to Philip, "Where will we be able to buy bread, so that these people can eat?" ⁶ (Now Yeshua said this to test Philip, for Yeshua himself knew what he was about to do.) ⁷ Philip answered, "Half a year's wages wouldn't buy enough bread for them — each one would get only a bite!" ⁸ One of the *talmidim*, Andrew the brother of Shim'on Kefa, said to him, ⁹ "There's a young fellow here who has five loaves of barley bread and two fish. But how far will they go among so many?" ¹⁰ Yeshua said, "Have the people sit down." There was a lot of grass there, so they sat down. The number of men was about five thousand. ¹¹ Then Yeshua took the loaves of bread, and, after making a *b'rakhah*, gave to all who were sitting there, and likewise with the fish, as much as they wanted. ¹² After they had eaten their fill, he told his *talmidim*, "Gather the leftover pieces, so that nothing gets wasted." ¹³ They gathered them and filled twelve baskets with the pieces from the five barley loaves left by those who had eaten.

¹⁴ When the people saw the miracle he had performed, they said, "This has to be 'the prophet' who is supposed to come into the world." ¹⁵ Yeshua knew that they were on the point of coming and seizing him, in order to make him king; so he went back to the hills again. This time he went by himself.

¹⁶ When evening came, his *talmidim* went down to the lake, ¹⁷ got into a boat and set out across the lake toward K'far-Nachum. By now it was dark, Yeshua had not yet joined them, ¹⁸ and the sea was getting rough, because a strong wind was blowing. ¹⁹ They had rowed three or four miles when they saw Yeshua approaching the boat, walking on the lake! They were terrified; ²⁰ but he said to them, "Stop being afraid, it is I." ²¹ Then they were willing to take him into the boat, and instantly the boat reached the land they were heading for.

²² The next day, the crowd which had stayed on the other side of the lake noticed that there had been only one boat there, and that Yeshua had not entered the boat with his *talmidim*, but that the *talmidim* had been alone when they sailed off. ²³ Then other boats, from Tiberias, came ashore near the place where they had eaten the bread after the Lord had made the *b'rakhah*. ²⁴ Accordingly, when the crowd saw that neither Yeshua nor his *talmidim*

were there, they themselves boarded the boats and made for K'far-Nachum in search of Yeshua.

²⁵ When they found him on the other side of the lake, they asked him, "Rabbi, when did you get here?" ²⁶ Yeshua answered, "Yes, indeed! I tell you, you're not looking for me because you saw miraculous signs, but because you ate the bread and had all you wanted! ²⁷ Don't work for the food which passes away but for the food that stays on into eternal life, which the Son of Man will give you. For this is the one on whom God the Father has put his seal."

²⁸ So they said to him, "What should we do in order to perform the works of God?" ²⁹ Yeshua answered, "Here's what the work of God is: to trust in the one he sent!"

³⁰ They said to him, "*Nu*, what miracle will you do for us, so that we may see it and trust you? What work can you perform? ³¹ Our fathers ate manna in the desert — as it says in the *Tanakh*, '**He gave them bread from heaven** to eat.'ᵈ ³² Yeshua said to them, "Yes, indeed! I tell you it wasn't Moshe who gave you the bread from heaven. But my Father is giving you the genuine bread from heaven; ³³ for God's bread is the one who comes down out of heaven and gives life to the world."

³⁴ They said to him, "Sir, give us this bread from now on." ³⁵ Yeshua answered, "I am the bread which is life! Whoever comes to me will never go hungry, and whoever trusts in me will never be thirsty. ³⁶ I told you that you have seen but still don't trust. ³⁷ Everyone the Father gives me will come to me, and whoever comes to me I will certainly not turn away. ³⁸ For I have come down from heaven to do not my

own will but the will of the one who sent me. ³⁹ And this is the will of the one who sent me: that I should not lose any of all those he has given me but should raise them up on the Last Day. ⁴⁰ Yes, this is the will of my Father: that all who see the Son and trust in him should have eternal life, and that I should raise them up on the Last Day."

⁴¹ At this the Judeans began grumbling about him because he said, "I am the bread which has come down from heaven." ⁴² They said, "Isn't this Yeshua Ben-Yosef? We know his father and mother! How can he now say, 'I have come down from heaven'?" ⁴³ Yeshua answered them, "Stop grumbling to each other! ⁴⁴ No one can come to me unless the Father — the one who sent me — draws him. And I will raise him up on the Last Day. ⁴⁵ It is written in the Prophets, '**They will all be taught by Adonai.**'ᵉ Everyone who listens to the Father and learns from him comes to me. ⁴⁶ Not that anyone has seen the Father except the one who is from God — he has seen the Father. ⁴⁷ Yes, indeed! I tell you, whoever trusts has eternal life: ⁴⁸ I am the bread which is life. ⁴⁹ Your fathers ate the manna in the desert; they died. ⁵⁰ But the bread that

---

e   Isaiah 54:13

A·do·**nai** — the LORD, Jehovah
b'ra·khah — blessing
K'far-Na·**chum** — Capernaum
Lake Kin·ne·ret — the Sea of Galilee
Mo·**she** — Moses
nu — if so
Pe·sach — Passover
Shim·'on Ke·**fa** — Simon Peter
tal·mi·dim — disciples
Ta·nakh — Hebrew Scriptures, "Old Testament"
Ye·**shu·a** — Jesus
Ye·shua Ben-Yo·**sef** — Jesus, son of Joseph

---

d   Psalm 78:24, Nehemiah 9:15

comes down from heaven is such that a person may eat it and not die. ⁵¹ I am the living bread that has come down from heaven; if anyone eats this bread, he will live forever. Furthermore, the bread that I will give is my own flesh; and I will give it for the life of the world."

⁵² At this, the Judeans disputed with one another, saying, "How can this man give us his flesh to eat?" ⁵³ Then Yeshua said to them, "Yes, indeed! I tell you that unless you eat the flesh of the Son of Man and drink his blood, you do not have life in yourselves. ⁵⁴ Whoever eats my flesh and drinks my blood has eternal life — that is, I will raise him up on the Last Day. ⁵⁵ For my flesh is true food, and my blood is true drink. ⁵⁶ Whoever eats my flesh and drinks my blood lives in me, and I live in him. ⁵⁷ Just as the living Father sent me, and I live through the Father, so also whoever eats me will live through me. ⁵⁸ So this is the bread that has come down from heaven — it is not like the bread the fathers ate; they're dead, but whoever eats this bread will live forever!" ⁵⁹ He said these things as he was teaching in a synagogue in K'far-Nachum.

⁶⁰ On hearing it, many of his *talmidim* said, "This is a hard word — who can bear to listen to it?" ⁶¹ But Yeshua, aware that his *talmidim* were grumbling about this, said to them, "This is a trap for you? ⁶² Suppose you were to see the Son of Man going back up to where he was before? ⁶³ It is the Spirit who gives life, the flesh is no help. The words I have spoken to you are Spirit and life, ⁶⁴ yet some among you do not trust." (For Yeshua knew from the outset which ones would not trust him, also which one would betray him.) ⁶⁵ "This," he said, "is why I told you that no one can come to me unless the Father has made it possible for him."

⁶⁶ From this time on, many of his *talmidim* turned back and no longer traveled around with him. ⁶⁷ So Yeshua said to the Twelve, "Don't you want to leave too?" ⁶⁸ Shim'on Kefa answered him, "Lord, to whom would we go? You have the word of eternal life. ⁶⁹ We have trusted, and we know that you are the Holy One of God." ⁷⁰ Yeshua answered them, "Didn't I choose you, the Twelve? Yet one of you is an adversary." ⁷¹ (He was speaking of Y'hudah Ben-Shim'on, from K'riot; for this man — one of the Twelve! — was soon to betray him.)

7 ¹ After this, Yeshua traveled around in the Galil, intentionally avoiding Y'hudah because the Judeans were out to kill him. ² But the festival of *Sukkot* in Y'hudah was near; ³ so his brothers said to him, "Leave here and go into Y'hudah, so that your *talmidim* can see the miracles you do; ⁴ for no one who wants to become known acts in secret. If you're doing these things, show yourself to the world!" ⁵ (His brothers spoke this way because they had not put their trust in him.) ⁶ Yeshua said to them, "My time has not yet come; but for you, any time is right. ⁷ The world can't hate you, but it does hate me, because I keep telling it how wicked its ways are. ⁸ You, go on up to the festival; as for me, I am not going up to this festival now, because the right time for me has not yet come." ⁹ Having said this, he stayed on in the Galil.

¹⁰ But after his brothers had gone up to the festival, he too went up, not publicly but in secret. ¹¹ At the festival, the Judeans were looking for him. "Where is he?" they asked. ¹² And among the crowds there was much whispering about him. Some said,

"He's a good man;" but others said, "No, he is deceiving the masses." 13 However, no one spoke about him openly, for fear of the Judeans. 14 Not until the festival was half over did Yeshua go up to the Temple courts and begin to teach. 15 The Judeans were surprised: "How does this man know so much without having studied?" they asked. 16 So Yeshua gave them an answer: "My teaching is not my own, it comes from the One who sent me. 17 If anyone wants to do his will, he will know whether my teaching is from God or I speak on my own. 18 A person who speaks on his own is trying to win praise for himself; but a person who tries to win praise for the one who sent him is honest, there is nothing false about him. 19 Didn't Moshe give you the *Torah*? Yet not one of you obeys the *Torah*! Why are you out to kill me?" 20 "You have a demon!" the crowd answered. "Who's out to kill you?" 21 Yeshua answered them, "I did one thing; and because of this, all of you are amazed. 22 Moshe gave you *b'rit-milah* — not that it came from Moshe but from the Patriarchs — and you do a boy's *b'rit-milah* on *Shabbat*. 23 If a boy is circumcised on *Shabbat* so that the *Torah* of Moshe will not be broken, why are you angry with me because I made a man's whole body well on *Shabbat*? 24 Stop judging by surface appearances, and judge the right way!"

25 Some of the Yerushalayim people said, "Isn't this the man they're out to kill? 26 Yet here he is, speaking openly; and they don't say anything to him. It couldn't be, could it, that the authorities have actually concluded he's the Messiah? 27 Surely not — we know where this man comes from; but when the Messiah comes, no one will know where he comes from." 28 Whereupon Yeshua, continuing to teach in the Temple courts, cried out, "Indeed you do know me! And you know where I'm from! And I have not come on my own! The One who sent me is real. But him you don't know! 29 I do know him, because I am with him, and he sent me!"

30 At this, they tried to arrest him; but no one laid a hand on him; because his time had not yet come. 31 However, many in the crowd put their trust in him and said, "When the Messiah comes, will he do more miracles than this man has done?"

32 The *P'rushim* heard the crowd whispering these things about Yeshua; so the head *cohanim* and the *P'rushim* sent some of the Temple guards to arrest him. 33 Yeshua said, "I will be with you only a little while longer; then I will go away to the One who sent me. 34 You will look for me and not find me; indeed, where I am, you cannot come." 35 The Judeans said to themselves, "Where is this man about to go, that we won't find him? Does he intend to go to the Greek Diaspora and teach the Greek-speaking Jews? 36 And when he says, 'You will look for me and not find

---

b'rit-mi·lah — circumcision
co·ha·nim — priests
the Ga·lil — Galilee
K'far-Na·chum — Capernaum
Mo·she — Moses
P'ru·shim — Pharisees
Shab·bat — the Sabbath
Shim·'on Ke·fa — Simon Peter
Suk·kot — Tabernacles
tal·mi·dim — disciples
To·rah — Teaching, "Law"; Pentateuch
Ye·ru·sha·la·yim — Jerusalem
Ye·shu·a — Jesus
Y'hu·dah — Judea
Y'hu·dah Ben-Shim·'on, from K'ri·ot — Judas the son of Simon Iscariot

me; indeed, where I am, you cannot come' — what does he mean?"

37 Now on the last day of the festival, *Hoshana Rabbah*, Yeshua stood and cried out, "If anyone is thirsty, let him keep coming to me and drinking! 38 Whoever puts his trust in me, as the Scripture says, rivers of living water will flow from his inmost being!" 39 (Now he said this about the Spirit, whom those who trusted in him were to receive later — the Spirit had not yet been given, because Yeshua had not yet been glorified.)

40 On hearing his words, some people in the crowd said, "Surely this man is 'the prophet';" 41 others said, "This is the Messiah." But others said, "How can the Messiah come from the Galil? 42 Doesn't the *Tanakh* say that the Messiah is from **the seed of David**[f] and comes **from Beit-Lechem,**[g] the village where David lived?" 43 So the people were divided because of him. 44 Some wanted to arrest him, but no one laid a hand on him.

45 The guards came back to the head *cohanim* and the *P'rushim*, who asked them, "Why didn't you bring him in?" 46 The guards replied, "No one ever spoke the way this man speaks!" 47 "You mean you've been taken in as well?" the *P'rushim* retorted. 48 "Has any of the authorities trusted him? Or any of the *P'rushim*? No! 49 True, these *am-ha'aretz* do, but they know nothing about the *Torah*, they are under a curse!"

50 Nakdimon, the man who had gone to Yeshua before and was one of them, said to them, 51 "Our *Torah* doesn't condemn a man — does it? — until after hearing from him and finding out what he's doing." 52 They replied, "You aren't from the Galil too, are you?

Study the *Tanakh*, and see for yourself that no prophet comes from the Galil!"

*53 Then they all left, each one to his own home.[1] But Yeshua went to the **8** Mount of Olives. 2 At daybreak, he appeared again in the Temple Court, where all the people gathered around him, and he sat down to teach them. 3 The *Torah*-teachers and the *P'rushim* brought in a woman who had been caught committing adultery and made her stand in the center of the group. 4 Then they said to him, "Rabbi, this woman was caught in the very act of committing adultery. 5 Now in our *Torah*, Moshe commanded that such a woman be stoned to death. What do you say about it?" 6 They said this to trap him, so that they might have ground for bringing charges against him; but Yeshua bent down and began writing in the dust with his finger. 7 When they kept questioning him, he straightened up and said to them, "The one of you who is without sin, let him be the first to throw a stone at her." 8 Then he bent down and wrote in the dust again. 9 On hearing this, they began to leave, one by one, the older ones first, until he was left alone, with the woman still there. 10 Standing up, Yeshua said to her, "Where are they? Has no one condemned you?" 11 She said, "No one, sir." Yeshua said, "Neither do I condemn you. Now go, and don't sin any more."

12 Yeshua spoke to them again: "I am the light of the world; whoever follows me will never walk in darkness but will have the light which gives life." 13 So the

---

f 2 Samuel 7:12   g Micah 5:1(2)

---

* Most scholars believe that 7:53-8:11, enclosed in brackets, is not from the pen of Yochanan. Many are of the opinion that it is a true story about Yeshua written by another of his disciples.

P'rushim said to him, "Now you're testifying on your own behalf; your testimony is not valid." ¹⁴ Yeshua answered them, "Even if I do testify on my own behalf, my testimony is indeed valid; because I know where I came from and where I'm going; but you do not know where I came from or where I'm going. ¹⁵ You judge by merely human standards. As for me, I pass judgment on no one; ¹⁶ but if I were indeed to pass judgment, my judgment would be valid; because it is not I alone who judge, but I and the one who sent me. ¹⁷ And even in your *Torah* it is written that the testimony of two people is valid. ¹⁸ I myself testify on my own behalf, and so does the Father who sent me."

¹⁹ They said to him, "Where is this 'father' of yours?" Yeshua answered, "You know neither me nor my Father; if you knew me, you would know my Father too." ²⁰ He said these things when he was teaching in the Temple treasury room; yet no one arrested him, because his time had not yet come.

²¹ Again he told them, "I am going away, and you will look for me, but you will die in your sin — where I am going, you cannot come." ²² The Judeans said, "Is he going to commit suicide? Is that what he means when he says, 'Where I am going, you cannot come'?" ²³ Yeshua said to them, "You are from below, I am from above; you are of this world, I am not of this world. ²⁴ This is why I said to you that you will die in your sins; for if you do not trust that I am who I say I am, you will die in your sins."

²⁵ At this, they said to him, "You? Who are you?" Yeshua answered, "Just what I've been telling you from the start. ²⁶ There are many things I could say about you, and many judgments I could make. However, the one who sent me is true; so I say in the world only what I have heard from him." ²⁷ They did not understand that he was talking to them about the Father. ²⁸ So Yeshua said, "When you lift up the Son of Man, then you will know that I am who I say I am, and that of myself I do nothing, but say only what the Father has taught me. ²⁹ Also, the One who sent me is still with me; he did not leave me to myself, because I always do what pleases him."

³⁰ Many people who heard him say these things trusted in him. ³¹ So Yeshua said to the Judeans who had trusted him, "If you obey what I say, then you are really my *talmidim*, ³² you will know the truth, and the truth will set you free." ³³ They answered, "We are the seed of Avraham and have never been slaves to anyone; so what do you mean by saying, 'You will be set free'?" ³⁴ Yeshua answered them, "Yes, indeed! I tell you that everyone who practices sin is a slave of sin. ³⁵ Now a slave does not remain with a family forever, but a son does remain with it forever. ³⁶ So if the Son frees you, you will really be free! ³⁷ I know you are the seed of Avraham. Yet you are out to kill me,

---

am-ha·'a·retz — ignorant masses
Av·ra·**ham** — Abraham
Beit-Le·chem — Bethlehem
co·ha·nim — priests
Da·**vid** — David
the Ga·**lil** — Galilee
Ho·sha·na Rab·bah — the greatest day
Mo·**she** — Moses
Nak·di·mon — Nicodemus
P'ru·shim — Pharisees
tal·mi·dim — disciples
Ta·nakh — Hebrew Scriptures, "Old Testament"
To·rah — Teaching, "Law"; Pentateuch
To·rah-teachers — scribes
Ye·shu·a — Jesus

14

because what I am saying makes no headway in you. ³⁸ I say what my Father has shown me; you do what your father has told you!"

³⁹ They answered him, "Our father is Avraham." Yeshua replied, "If you are children of Avraham, then do the things Avraham did! ⁴⁰ As it is, you are out to kill me, a man who has told you the truth which I heard from God. Avraham did nothing like that! ⁴¹ You are doing the things your father does." "We're not illegitimate children!" they said to him. "We have only one Father — God!" ⁴² Yeshua replied to them, "If God were your Father, you would love me; because I came out from God; and now I have arrived here. I did not come on my own; he sent me. ⁴³ Why don't you understand what I'm saying? Because you can't bear to listen to my message. ⁴⁴ You belong to your father, Satan, and you want to carry out your father's desires. From the start he was a murderer, and he has never stood by the truth, because there is no truth in him. When he tells a lie, he is speaking in character; because he is a liar — indeed, the inventor of the lie! ⁴⁵ But as for me, because I tell the truth you don't believe me. ⁴⁶ Which one of you can show me where I'm wrong? If I'm telling the truth, why don't you believe me? ⁴⁷ Whoever belongs to God listens to what God says; the reason you don't listen is that you don't belong to God."

⁴⁸ The Judeans answered him, "Aren't we right in saying you are from Shomron and have a demon?" ⁴⁹ Yeshua replied, "Me? I have no demon. I am honoring my Father. But you dishonor me. ⁵⁰ I am not seeking praise for myself. There is one who is seeking it, and he is the judge. ⁵¹ Yes, indeed! I tell you that whoever obeys my teaching will never see death."

⁵² The Judeans said to him, "Now we know for sure that you have a demon! Avraham died, and so did the prophets; yet you say, 'Whoever obeys my teaching will never taste death.' ⁵³ *Avraham avinu* died; you aren't greater than he, are you? And the prophets also died. Who do you think you are?" ⁵⁴ Yeshua answered, "If I praise myself, my praise counts for nothing. The one who is praising me is my Father, the very one about whom you keep saying, 'He is our God.' ⁵⁵ Now you have not known him, but I do know him; indeed, if I were to say that I don't know him, I would be a liar like you! But I do know him, and I obey his word. ⁵⁶ Avraham, your father, was glad that he would see my day; then he saw it and was overjoyed."

⁵⁷ "Why, you're not yet fifty years old," the Judeans replied, "and you have seen Avraham?" ⁵⁸ Yeshua said to them, "Yes, indeed! Before Avraham came into being, I AM!" ⁵⁹ At this, they picked up stones to throw at him; but Yeshua was hidden and left the Temple grounds.

9 ¹ As Yeshua passed along, he saw a man blind from birth. ² His *talmidim* asked him, "Rabbi, who sinned — this man or his parents — to cause him to be born blind?" ³ Yeshua answered, "His blindness is due neither to his sin nor to that of his parents; it happened so that God's power might be seen at work in him. ⁴ As long as it is day, we must keep doing the work of the One who sent me; the night is coming, when no one can work. ⁵ While I am in the world, I am the light of the world."

⁶ Having said this, he spit on the ground, made some mud with the saliva, put the mud on the man's eyes, ⁷ and said to him, "Go, wash off in the Pool of Shiloach!" (The name means "sent".) So he went and washed and came away seeing.

15

⁸ His neighbors and those who previously had seen him begging said, "Isn't this the man who used to sit and beg?" ⁹ Some said, "Yes, he's the one;" while others said, "No, but he looks like him." However, he himself said, "I'm the one." ¹⁰ "How were your eyes opened?" they asked him. ¹¹ He answered, "The man called Yeshua made mud, put it on my eyes, and told me, 'Go to Shiloach and wash!' So I went; and as soon as I had washed, I could see." ¹² They said to him, "Where is he?" and he replied, "I don't know."

¹³ They took the man who had been blind to the *P'rushim*. ¹⁴ Now the day on which Yeshua had made the mud and opened his eyes was *Shabbat*. ¹⁵ So the *P'rushim* asked him again how he had become able to see; and he told them, "He put mud on my eyes, then I washed, and now I can see." ¹⁶ At this, some of the *P'rushim* said, "This man is not from God, because he doesn't keep *Shabbat*." But others said, "How could a man who is a sinner do miracles like these?" And there was a split among them. ¹⁷ So once more they spoke to the blind man: "Since you're the one whose eyes he opened, what do you say about him?" He replied: "He is a prophet."

¹⁸ The Judeans, however, were unwilling to believe that he had formerly been blind, but now could see, until they had summoned the man's parents. ¹⁹ They asked them, "Is this your son, who you say was born blind? How is it that now he can see?" ²⁰ His parents answered, "We know that this is our son and that he was born blind; ²¹ but how it is that he can see now, we don't know; nor do we know who opened his eyes. Ask him — he's old enough, he can speak for himself!" ²² The parents said this because they were afraid of the Judeans, for the Judeans had already agreed that anyone who acknowledged Yeshua as the Messiah would be banned from the synagogue. ²³ This is why his parents said, "He's old enough, ask him."

²⁴ So a second time they called the man who had been blind; and they said to him, "Swear to God that you will tell the truth! We know that this man is a sinner." ²⁵ He answered, "Whether he's a sinner or not I don't know. One thing I do know: I was blind, now I see." ²⁶ So they said to him, "What did he do to you? How did he open your eyes?" ²⁷ "I already told you," he answered, "and you didn't listen. Why do you want to hear it again? Maybe you too want to become his *talmidim*?" ²⁸ Then they railed at him. "You may be his *talmid*," they said, "but we are *talmidim* of Moshe! ²⁹ We know that God has spoken to Moshe, but as for this fellow — we don't know where he's from!" ³⁰ "What a strange thing," the man answered, "that you don't know where he's from — considering that he opened my eyes! ³¹ We know that God doesn't listen to sinners; but if anyone fears God and does his will, God does listen to him. ³² In all history no one has ever heard of someone's opening the eyes of a man born blind. ³³ If this man were not from God, he couldn't do a thing!" ³⁴ "Why, you *mamzer*!" they retorted, "Are you lecturing us?" And they threw him out.

Av·ra·**ham** — Abraham
*Av·ra·**ham** a·vi·nu* — our father, Abraham
*mam·**zer*** — bastard, born in sin
Mo·she — Moses
P'ru·shim — Pharisees
Sa·tan — Satan
*Shab·**bat*** — the Sabbath
Shi·lo·ach — Siloam
Shom·ron — Samaria
*tal·**mid*** (pl. *tal·mi·dim*) — disciple
Ye·shu·a — Jesus

35 Yeshua heard that they had thrown the man out. He found him and said, "Do you trust in the Son of Man?" 36 "Sir," he answered, "tell me who he is, so that I can trust in him." 37 Yeshua said to him, "You have seen him. In fact, he's the one speaking with you now." 38 "Lord, I trust!" he said, and he kneeled down in front of him.

39 Yeshua said, "It is to judge that I came into this world, so that those who do not see might see, and those who do see might become blind." 40 Some of the *P'rushim* nearby heard this and said to him, "So we're blind too, are we?" 41 Yeshua answered them, "If you were blind, you would not be guilty of sin. But since you still say, 'We see,' your guilt remains.

10 1 "Yes, indeed! I tell you, the person who doesn't enter the sheep-pen through the door, but climbs in some other way, is a thief and a robber. 2 But the one who goes in through the gate is the sheep's own shepherd. 3 This is the one the gate-keeper admits, and the sheep hear his voice. He calls his own sheep, each one by name, and leads them out. 4 After taking out all that are his own, he goes on ahead of them; and the sheep follow him because they recognize his voice. 5 They never follow a stranger but will run away from him, because strangers' voices are unfamiliar to them."

6 Yeshua used this indirect manner of speaking with them, but they didn't understand what he was talking to them about. 7 So Yeshua said to them again, "Yes, indeed! I tell you that I am the gate for the sheep. 8 All those who have come before me have been thieves and robbers, but the sheep didn't listen to them. 9 I am the gate; if someone enters through me, he will be safe and will go in and out and find pasture. 10 The thief comes only in order to steal, kill and destroy; I have come so that they may have life, life in its fullest measure.

11 "I am the good shepherd. The good shepherd lays down his life for the sheep. 12 The hired hand, since he isn't a shepherd and the sheep aren't his own, sees the wolf coming, abandons the sheep and runs away. Then the wolf drags them off and scatters them. 13 The hired worker behaves like this because that's all he is, a hired worker; so it doesn't matter to him what happens to the sheep. 14 I am the good shepherd; I know my own, and my own know me — 15 just as the Father knows me, and I know the Father — and I lay down my life on behalf of the sheep. 16 Also I have other sheep which are not from this pen; I need to bring them, and they will hear my voice; and there will be one flock, one shepherd.

17 "This is why the Father loves me: because I lay down my life — in order to take it up again! 18 No one takes it away from me; on the contrary, I lay it down of my own free will. I have the power to lay it down, and I have the power to take it up again. This is what my Father commanded me to do."

19 Again there was a split among the Judeans because of what he said. 20 Many of them said, "He has a demon!" and "He's *meshugga*! Why do you listen to him?" 21 Others said, "These are not the deeds of a man who is demonized — how can a demon open blind people's eyes?"

22 Then came *Chanukkah* in Yerushalayim. It was winter, 23 and Yeshua was walking around inside the Temple area, in Shlomo's Colonnade. 24 So the Judeans surrounded him and said to him, "How much longer are you going to keep us in suspense? If you are the Messiah, tell us publicly!" 25 Yeshua answered them, "I have already told

you, and you don't trust me. The works I do in my Father's name testify on my behalf; ²⁶ but the reason you don't trust is that you are not included among my sheep. ²⁷ My sheep listen to my voice, I recognize them, they follow me, ²⁸ and I give them eternal life. They will absolutely never be destroyed, and no one will snatch them from my hands. ²⁹ My Father, who gave them to me, is greater than all; and no one can snatch from the Father's hands. ³⁰ I and the Father are one."

³¹ Once again the Judeans picked up rocks in order to stone him. ³² Yeshua answered them, "You have seen me do many good deeds that reflect the Father's power; for which one of these deeds are you stoning me?" ³³ The Judeans replied, "We are not stoning you for any good deed, but for blasphemy — because you, who are only a man, are making yourself out to be God [*Elohim*]." ³⁴ Yeshua answered them, "Isn't it written in your *Torah*, '**You people are *Elohim***'?ʰ ³⁵ If he called '*Elohim*' the people to whom the word of *Elohim* was addressed (and the *Tanakh* cannot be broken), ³⁶ then are you telling the one whom the Father set apart as holy and sent into the world, 'You are committing blasphemy,' just because I said, 'I am a son of *Elohim*'? ³⁷ "If I am not doing deeds that reflect my Father's power, don't trust me. ³⁸ But if I am, then, even if you don't trust me, trust the deeds; so that you may understand once and for all that the Father is united with me, and I am united with the Father." ³⁹ One more time they tried to arrest him, but he slipped out of their hands.

⁴⁰ He went off again beyond the Yarden, where Yochanan had been immersing at first, and stayed there.

⁴¹ Many people came to him and said, "Yochanan performed no miracles, but everything Yochanan said about this man was true." ⁴² And many people there put their trust in him.

11 ¹There was a man who had fallen sick. His name was El'azar, and he came from Beit-Anyah, the village where Miryam and her sister Marta lived. ²(This Miryam, whose brother El'azar had become sick, is the one who poured perfume on the Lord and wiped his feet with her hair.) ³ So the sisters sent a message to Yeshua, "Lord, the man you love is sick." ⁴ On hearing it, he said, "This sickness will not end in death. No, it is for God's glory, so that the Son of God may receive glory through it."

⁵ Yeshua loved Marta and her sister and El'azar; ⁶ so when he heard he was sick, first he stayed where he was two more days; ⁷ then, after this, he said to the *talmidim*, "Let's go back to Y'hudah." ⁸ The *talmidim* replied, "Rabbi! Just a short while ago the Judeans were out to stone you — and you want to go back there?" ⁹ Yeshua

---

Beit-An·**yah** — Bethany
Cha·nuk·kah — the Feast of Dedication
El·'a·**zar** — Lazarus
E·lo·him — God, gods
Mar·ta — Martha
me·shug·ga — crazy
Mir·**yam** — Miriam, Mary
P'ru·shim — Pharisees
Shlo·**mo** — Solomon
tal·mi·dim — disciples
Ta·nakh — Hebrew Scriptures, "Old Testament"
To·rah — Teaching, "Law"; Pentateuch
Yar·den — Jordan
Ye·ru·sha·**la·yim** — Jerusalem
Ye·**shu**·a — Jesus
Y'hu·**dah** — Judea
Yo·cha·**nan** — John

ʰ Psalm 82:6

answered, "Aren't there twelve hours of daylight? If a person walks during daylight, he doesn't stumble; because he sees the light of this world. ¹⁰ But if a person walks at night, he does stumble; because he has no light with him."

¹¹ Yeshua said these things, and afterwards he said to the *talmidim*, "Our friend El'azar has gone to sleep; but I am going in order to wake him up." ¹² The *talmidim* said to him, "Lord, if he has gone to sleep, he will get better." ¹³ Now Yeshua had used the phrase to speak about El'azar's death, but they thought he had been talking literally about sleep. ¹⁴ So Yeshua told them in plain language, "El'azar has died. ¹⁵ And for your sakes, I am glad that I wasn't there, so that you may come to trust. But let's go to him." ¹⁶ Then T'oma (the name means "twin") said to his fellow *talmidim*, "Yes, we should go, so that we can die with him!"

¹⁷ On arrival, Yeshua found that El'azar had already been in the tomb for four days. ¹⁸ Now Beit-Anyah was about two miles from Yerushalayim, ¹⁹ and many of the Judeans had come to Marta and Miryam in order to comfort them at the loss of their brother. ²⁰ So when Marta heard that Yeshua was coming, she went out to meet him; but Miryam continued sitting *shiv'ah* in the house.

²¹ Marta said to Yeshua, "Lord, if you had been here, my brother would not have died. ²² Even now I know that whatever you ask of God, God will give you." ²³ Yeshua said to her, "Your brother will rise again." ²⁴ Marta said, "I know that he will rise again at the Resurrection on the Last Day." ²⁵ Yeshua said to her, "I AM the Resurrection and the Life! Whoever puts his trust in me will live, even if he dies; ²⁶ and everyone living and trusting in me will never die. Do you believe this?"

²⁷ She said to him, "Yes, Lord, I believe that you are the Messiah, the Son of God, the one coming into the world."

²⁸ After saying this, she went off and secretly called Miryam, her sister: "The Rabbi is here and is calling for you." ²⁹ When she heard this, she jumped up and went to him. ³⁰ Yeshua had not yet come into the village but was still where Marta had met him; ³¹ so when the Judeans who had been with Miryam in the house comforting her saw her get up quickly and go out, they followed her, thinking she was going to the tomb to mourn there.

³² When Miryam came to where Yeshua was and saw him, she fell at his feet and said to him, "Lord, if you had been here, my brother would not have died." ³³ When Yeshua saw her crying, and also the Judeans who came with her crying, he was deeply moved and also troubled. ³⁴ He said, "Where have you buried him?" They said, "Lord, come and see." ³⁵ Yeshua cried; ³⁶ so the Judeans there said, "See how he loved him!" ³⁷ But some of them said, "He opened the blind man's eyes. Couldn't he have kept this one from dying?"

³⁸ Yeshua, again deeply moved, came to the tomb. It was a cave, and a stone was lying in front of the entrance. ³⁹ Yeshua said, "Take the stone away!" Marta, the sister of the dead man, said to Yeshua, "By now his body must smell, for it has been four days since he died!" ⁴⁰ Yeshua said to her, "Didn't I tell you that if you keep trusting, you will see the glory of God?" ⁴¹ So they removed the stone. Yeshua looked upward and said, "Father, I thank you that you have heard me. ⁴² I myself know that you always hear me, but I say this because of the crowd standing around, so that they may believe that you have sent me." ⁴³ Having said this, he shouted, "El'azar! Come out!" ⁴⁴ The

man who had been dead came out, his hands and feet wrapped in strips of linen and his face covered with a cloth. Yeshua said to them, "Unwrap him, and let him go!" ⁴⁵ At this, many of the Judeans who had come to visit Miryam, and had seen what Yeshua had done, trusted in him.

⁴⁶ But some of them went off to the *P'rushim* and told them what he had done. ⁴⁷ So the head *cohanim* and the *P'rushim* called a meeting of the *Sanhedrin* and said, "What are we going to do? — for this man is performing many miracles. ⁴⁸ If we let him keep going on this way, everyone will trust in him, and the Romans will come and destroy both the Temple and the nation." ⁴⁹ But one of them, Kayafa, who was *cohen gadol* that year, said to them, "You people don't know anything! ⁵⁰ You don't see that it's better for you if one man dies on behalf of the people, so that the whole nation won't be destroyed." ⁵¹ Now he didn't speak this way on his own initiative; rather, since he was *cohen gadol* that year, he was prophesying that Yeshua was about to die on behalf of the nation, ⁵² and not for the nation alone, but so that he might gather into one the scattered children of God.

⁵³ From that day on, they made plans to have him put to death. ⁵⁴ Therefore Yeshua no longer walked around openly among the Judeans but went away from there into the region near the desert, to a town called Efrayim, and stayed there with his *talmidim*.

⁵⁵ The Judean festival of *Pesach* was near, and many people went up from the country to Yerushalayim to perform the purification ceremony prior to *Pesach*. ⁵⁶ They were looking for Yeshua, and as they stood in the Temple courts they said to each other, "What do you think? That he simply won't come to the festival?" ⁵⁷ Moreover, the head *cohanim* and the *P'rushim* had given orders that anyone knowing Yeshua's whereabouts should inform them, so that they could have him arrested.

12 ¹ Six days before *Pesach*, Yeshua came to Beit-Anyah, where El'azar lived, the man Yeshua had raised from the dead; ² so they gave a dinner there in his honor. Marta served the meal, and El'azar was among those at the table with him. ³ Miryam took a whole pint of pure oil of spikenard, which is very expensive, poured it on Yeshua's feet and wiped his feet with her hair, so that the house was filled with the fragrance of the perfume. ⁴ But one of the *talmidim*, Y'hudah from K'riot, the one who was about to betray him, said, ⁵ "This perfume is worth a year's wages! Why wasn't it sold and the money given to the poor?" ⁶ Now he said this not out of concern for the poor, but because he was a thief — he was in charge of the common purse and used to steal from it. ⁷ Yeshua said, "Leave her alone! She kept this for the day of my burial. ⁸ You always have the

---

Beit-An·**yah** — Bethany
co·ha·nim — priests
co·hen ga·dol — high priest
Ef·**ra**·yim — Ephraim
El·'**a**·**zar** — Lazarus
Ka·ya·**fa** — Caiaphas
Mar·ta — Martha
Mir·yam — Miriam, Mary
Pe·sach — Passover
P'ru·shim — Pharisees
San·**hed**·**rin** — Jewish religious court
sitting *shiv·'ah* — mourning
tal·mi·dim — disciples
T·'**o**·ma — Thomas
Ye·ru·sha·**la**·yim — Jerusalem
Ye·**shu**·a — Jesus
Y'hu·dah from K'ri·ot — Judas Iscariot

poor among you, but you will not always have me."

[9] A large crowd of Judeans learned that he was there; and they came not only because of Yeshua, but also so that they could see El'azar, whom he had raised from the dead. [10] The head *cohanim* then decided to do away with El'azar too, [11] since it was because of him that large numbers of the Judeans were leaving their leaders and putting their trust in Yeshua.

[12] The next day, the large crowd that had come for the festival heard that Yeshua was on his way into Yerushalayim. [13] They took palm branches and went out to meet him, shouting,

"Deliver us!"[i]

"Blessed is he who comes in the name of *Adonai*,[j] the King of Israel!"

[14] After finding a donkey colt, Yeshua mounted it, just as the *Tanakh* says —

[15] **"Daughter of Tziyon, don't be afraid!
Look! Your King is coming, sitting on a donkey's colt."**[k]

[16] His *talmidim* did not understand this at first; but after Yeshua had been glorified, then they remembered that the *Tanakh* said this about him, and that they had done this for him. [17] The group that had been with him when he called El'azar out of the tomb and raised him from the dead had been telling about it. [18] It was because of this too that the crowd came out to meet him — they had heard that he had performed this miracle. [19] The *P'rushim* said to each other, "Look, you're getting nowhere! Why, the whole world has gone after him!"

[20] Among those who went up to worship at the festival were some Greek-speaking Jews. [21] They approached Philip, the one from Beit-Tzaidah in the Galil, with a request. "Sir," they said, "we would like to see Yeshua." [22] Philip came and told Andrew; then Andrew and Philip went and told Yeshua. [23] Yeshua gave them this answer: "The time has come for the Son of Man to be glorified. [24] Yes, indeed! I tell you that unless a grain of wheat that falls to the ground dies, it stays just a grain; but if it dies, it produces a big harvest. [25] He who loves his life loses it, but he who hates his life in this world will keep it safe right on into eternal life! [26] If someone is serving me, let him follow me; wherever I am, my servant will be there too. My Father will honor anyone who serves me.

[27] "Now I am in turmoil. What can I say — 'Father, save me from this hour'? No, it was for this very reason that I have come to this hour. I will say this: [28] Father, glorify your name!" At this a *bat-kol* came out of heaven, "I have glorified it before, and I will glorify it again!" [29] The crowd standing there and hearing it said that it had thundered; others said, "An angel spoke to him." [30] Yeshua answered, "This *bat-kol* did not come for my sake but for yours. [31] Now is the time for this world to be judged, now the ruler of this world will be expelled. [32] As for me, when I am lifted up from the earth, I will draw everyone to myself." [33] He said this to indicate what kind of death he would die.

[34] The crowd answered, "We have learned from the *Torah* that the Messiah remains forever. How is it that you say the Son of Man has to be 'lifted up'? Who is this 'Son of Man'?" [35] Yeshua said to them, "The light will be with you only a little while longer.

---

i Psalm 118:25   *j* Psalm 118:26
k Zechariah 9:9

Walk while you have the light, or the dark will overtake you; he who walks in the dark doesn't know where he's going. ³⁶ While you have the light, put your trust in the light, so that you may become people of light." Yeshua said these things, then went off and kept himself hidden from them.

³⁷ Even though he had performed so many miracles in their presence, they still did not put their trust in him, ³⁸ in order that what Yesha'yahu the prophet had said might be fulfilled,

"*Adonai*, who has believed our report?
To whom has the arm of *Adonai* been revealed?"*ˡ*

³⁹ The reason they could not believe was — as Yesha'yahu said elsewhere —

⁴⁰ "He has blinded their eyes
and hardened their hearts,
so that they do not see with their eyes,
understand with their hearts,
or turn from their sins
for me to heal them."*ᵐ*

⁴¹ (Yesha'yahu said these things because he saw the *Sh'khinah* of Yeshua and spoke about him.) ⁴² Nevertheless, many of the leaders did trust in him; but because of the *P'rushim* they did not say so openly, out of fear of being banned from the synagogue; ⁴³ for they loved praise from other people more than praise from God.

⁴⁴ Yeshua declared publicly, "Those who put their trust in me are trusting not merely in me, but in the One who sent me. ⁴⁵ Also those who see me see the One who sent me. ⁴⁶ I have come as a light into the world, so that everyone who trusts in me might not remain in the dark. ⁴⁷ If anyone hears what I am

saying and does not observe it, I don't judge him; for I did not come to judge the world, but to save the world. ⁴⁸ Those who reject me and don't accept what I say have a judge — the word which I have spoken will judge them on the Last Day. ⁴⁹ For I have not spoken on my own initiative; but the Father who sent me has given me a command, namely, what to say and how to say it. ⁵⁰ And I know that his command is eternal life. So what I say is simply what the Father has told me to say."

13 ¹ It was just before the festival of *Pesach*, and Yeshua knew that the time had come for him to pass from this world to the Father. Having loved his own people in the world, he loved them to the end. ² They were at supper, and the Adversary had already put the desire to betray him into the heart of Y'hudah Ben-Shim'on from K'riot. ³ Yeshua was aware that the Father had put everything in his power, and that he had come from God and was returning to God. ⁴ So he rose from the table, removed his outer garments and

---

A·do·nai — the LORD, Jehovah
bat-kol — heavenly voice
Beit-Za·ta — Bethzatha
co·ha·nim — priests
El·'a·zar — Lazarus
the *Ga·lil* — Galilee
P'ru·shim — Pharisees
Pe·sach — Passover
Sh'khi • nah — God's manifest glory
tal·mi·dim — disciples
Ta·nakh — Hebrew Scriptures, "Old Testament"
To·rah — Teaching, "Law"; Pentateuch
Tzi·yon — Zion
Ye·ru·sha·la·yim — Jerusalem
Ye·sha'·ya·hu — Isaiah
Ye·shu·a — Jesus
Y'hu·dah Ben-Shim·'on, from K'ri·ot — Judas the son of Simon Iscariot

---

ˡ Isaiah 53:1   *ᵐ* Isaiah 6:10

wrapped a towel around his waist.
⁵Then he poured some water into a
basin and began to wash the feet of the
talmidim and wipe them off with the
towel wrapped around him.
⁶ He came to Shim'on Kefa, who said
to him, "Lord! You are washing my
feet?" ⁷Yeshua answered him, "You
don't understand yet what I am doing,
but in time you will understand."
⁸ "No!" said Kefa, "you will never wash
my feet!" Yeshua answered him, "If I
don't wash you, you have no share with
me." ⁹ "Lord," Shim'on Kefa replied,
"not only my feet, but my hands and
head too!" ¹⁰Yeshua said to him, "A
man who has had a bath doesn't need
to wash, except his feet — his body is
already clean. And you people are
clean, but not all of you." ¹¹(He knew
who was betraying him; this is why he
said, "Not all of you are clean.")
¹²After he had washed their feet,
taken back his clothes and returned to
the table, he said to them, "Do you
understand what I have done to you?
¹³You call me 'Rabbi' and 'Lord,' and
you are right, because I am. ¹⁴Now if I,
the Lord and Rabbi, have washed your
feet, you also should wash each other's
feet. ¹⁵For I have set you an example,
so that you may do as I have done to
you. ¹⁶Yes, indeed! I tell you, a slave is
not greater than his master, nor is an
emissary greater than the one who sent
him. ¹⁷If you know these things, you
will be blessed if you do them.
¹⁸ "I'm not talking to all of you — I
know which ones I have chosen. But
the words of the *Tanakh* must be
fulfilled that say, '**The one eating my
bread has turned against me.**'ⁿ ¹⁹I'm
telling you now, before it happens; so
that when it does happen, you may
believe that I AM who I say I am. ²⁰Yes,

indeed! I tell you that a person who
receives someone I send receives me,
and that anyone who receives me
receives the One who sent me.
²¹After saying this, Yeshua, in deep
anguish of spirit, declared, "Yes,
indeed! I tell you that one of you will
betray me.' ²²The *talmidim* stared at
one another, totally mystified — whom
could he mean? ²³One of his *talmidim*,
the one Yeshua particularly loved, was
reclining close beside him. ²⁴So Shim'on
Kefa motioned to him and said, "Ask
which one he's talking about." ²⁵Lean-
ing against Yeshua's chest, he asked
Yeshua, "Lord, who is it?" ²⁶Yeshua
answered, "It's the one to whom I give
this piece of *matzah* after I dip it in the
dish." So he dipped the piece of *matzah*
and gave it to Y'hudah Ben-Shim'on
from K'riot. ²⁷As soon as Y'hudah took
the piece of *matzah*, the Adversary
went into him. "What you are doing,
do quickly!" Yeshua said to him. ²⁸But
no one at the table understood why he
had said this to him. ²⁹Some thought
that since Y'hudah was in charge of the
common purse, Yeshua was telling him,
"Buy what we need for the festival," or
telling him to give something to the
poor. ³⁰As soon as he had taken the
piece of *matzah*, Y'hudah went out,
and it was night.
³¹After Y'hudah had left, Yeshua
said, "Now the Son of Man has been
glorified, and God has been glorified in
him. ³²If the Son has glorified God,
God will himself glorify the Son, and
will do so without delay. ³³Little children, I will be with you only a little
longer. You will look for me; and, as I
said to the Judeans, 'Where I am going,
you cannot come,' now I say it to you
as well.
³⁴ "I am giving you a new command:
that you keep on loving each other. In
the same way that I have loved you,

ⁿ Psalm 41:10(9)

you are also to keep on loving each other. ³⁵Everyone will know that you are my *talmidim* by the fact that you have love for each other."

³⁶Shim'on Kefa said to him, "Lord, where are you going?" Yeshua answered, "Where I am going, you cannot follow me now; but you will follow later." ³⁷"Lord," Kefa said to him, "why can't I follow you now? I will lay down my life for you!" ³⁸Yeshua answered, "You will lay down your life for me? Yes, indeed! I tell you, before the rooster crows you will disown me three times. ¹Don't let yourselves be disturbed. Trust in God and trust in me. ²In my Father's house are many places to live. If there weren't, I would have told you; because I am going there to prepare a place for you. ³Since I am going and preparing a place for you, I will return to take you with me; so that where I am, you may be also. ⁴Furthermore, you know where I'm going; and you know the way there."

⁵T'oma said to him, "Lord, we don't know where you're going; so how can we know the way?" ⁶Yeshua said, "I AM the Way — and the Truth and the Life; no one comes to the Father except through me. ⁷Because you have known me, you will also know my Father; from now on, you do know him — in fact, you have seen him."

⁸Philip said to him, "Lord, show us the Father, and it will be enough for us." ⁹Yeshua replied to him, "Have I been with you so long without your knowing me, Philip? Whoever has seen me has seen the Father; so how can you say, 'Show us the Father'? ¹⁰Don't you believe that I am united with the Father, and the Father united with me? What I am telling you, I am not saying on my own initiative; the Father living in me is doing his own works. ¹¹Trust me, that I

am united with the Father, and the Father united with me. But if you can't, then trust because of the works themselves.

¹²"Yes, indeed! I tell you that whoever trusts in me will also do the works I do! Indeed, he will do greater ones, because I am going to the Father. ¹³In fact, whatever you ask for in my name, I will do; so that the Father may be glorified in the Son. ¹⁴If you ask me for something in my name, I will do it.

¹⁵"If you love me, you will keep my commands; ¹⁶and I will ask the Father, and he will give you another comforting Counselor like me, the Spirit of Truth, to be with you forever. ¹⁷The world cannot receive him, because it neither sees nor knows him. You know him, because he is staying with you and will be united with you. ¹⁸I will not leave you orphans — I am coming to you. ¹⁹In just a little while, the world will no longer see me; but you will see me. Because I live, you too will live. ²⁰When that day comes, you will know that I am united with my Father, and you with me, and I with you. ²¹Whoever has my commands and keeps them is the one who loves me, and the one who loves me will be loved by my Father, and I will love him and reveal myself to him."

²²Y'hudah (not the one from K'riot) said to him, "What has happened,

---

Ke·**fa** — Peter

ma·tzah — unleavened bread

Shim·'on Ke·**fa** — Simon Peter

tal·mi·dim — disciples

Ta·nakh — Hebrew Scriptures, "Old Testament"

T·'o·ma — Thomas

Ye·shu·a — Jesus

Y'hu·**dah** (not the one from K'ri·ot) — Judas (not Iscariot)

Y'hu·**dah** Ben-Shim·'on, from K'ri·ot — Judas the son of Simon Iscariot

Lord, that you are about to reveal yourself to us and not to the world?" ²³Yeshua answered him, "If someone loves me, he will keep my word; and my Father will love him, and we will come to him and make our home with him. ²⁴Someone who doesn't love me doesn't keep my words — and the word you are hearing is not my own but that of the Father who sent me.

²⁵"I have told you these things while I am still with you. ²⁶But the Counselor, the *Ruach HaKodesh*, whom the Father will send in my name, will teach you everything; that is, he will remind you of everything I have said to you. ²⁷"What I am leaving with you is *shalom* — I am giving you my *shalom*. I don't give the way the world gives. Don't let yourselves be upset or frightened. ²⁸You heard me tell you, 'I am leaving, and I will come back to you.' If you loved me, you would have been glad that I am going to the Father; because the Father is greater than I. ²⁹Also, I have said it to you now, before it happens; so that when it does happen, you will trust.

³⁰"I won't be talking with you much longer, because the ruler of this world is coming. He has no claim on me; ³¹rather, this is happening so that the world may know that I love the Father, and that I do as the Father has commanded me.

"Get up! Let's get going!"

15 ¹"I am the real vine, and my Father is the gardener. ²Every branch which is part of me but fails to bear fruit, he cuts off; and every branch that does bear fruit, he prunes, so that it may bear more fruit. ³Right now, because of the word which I have spoken to you, you are pruned. ⁴Stay united with me, as I will with you — for just as the branch can't put forth fruit by itself apart from the vine, so you can't bear fruit apart from me.

⁵"I am the vine and you are the branches. Those who stay united with me, and I with them, are the ones who bear much fruit; because apart from me you can't do a thing. ⁶Unless a person remains united with me, he is thrown away like a branch and dries up. Such branches are gathered and thrown into the fire, where they are burned up.

⁷"If you remain united with me, and my words with you, then ask whatever you want, and it will happen for you. ⁸This is how my Father is glorified — in your bearing much fruit; this is how you will prove to be my *talmidim*.

⁹"Just as my Father has loved me, I too have loved you; so stay in my love. ¹⁰If you keep my commands, you will stay in my love — just as I have kept my Father's commands and stay in his love. ¹¹I have said this to you so that my joy may be in you, and your joy be complete.

¹²"This is my command: that you keep on loving each other just as I have loved you. ¹³No one has greater love than a person who lays down his life for his friends. ¹⁴You are my friends, if you do what I command you. ¹⁵I no longer call you slaves, because a slave doesn't know what his master is about; but I have called you friends, because everything I have heard from my Father I have made known to you. ¹⁶You did not choose me, I chose you; and I have commissioned you to go and bear fruit, fruit that will last; so that whatever you ask from the Father in my name he may give you. ¹⁷This is what I command you: keep loving each other!

¹⁸"If the world hates you, under-

stand that it hated me first. ¹⁹If you belonged to the world, the world would have loved its own. But because you do not belong to the world — on the contrary, I have picked you out of the world — therefore the world hates you. ²⁰Remember what I told you, 'A slave is not greater than his master.' If they persecuted me, they will persecute you too; if they kept my word, they will keep yours too. ²¹But they will do all this to you on my account, because they don't know the One who sent me.

²²"If I had not come and spoken to them, they wouldn't be guilty of sin; but now, they have no excuse for their sin. ²³Whoever hates me hates my Father also. ²⁴If I had not done in their presence works which no one else ever did, they would not be guilty of sin; but now, they have seen them and have hated both me and my Father. ²⁵But this has happened in order to fulfill the words in their *Torah* which read, '**They hated me for no reason at all.**'ᵒ

²⁶"When the Counselor comes, whom I will send you from the Father — the Spirit of Truth, who keeps going out from the Father — he will testify on my behalf. ²⁷And you testify too, because you have been with me from the outset.

16 ¹"I have told you these things so that you won't be caught by surprise. ²They will ban you from the synagogue; in fact, the time will come when anyone who kills you will think he is serving God! ³They will do these things because they have understood neither the Father nor me. ⁴But I have told you this, so that when the time comes for it to happen, you will remember that I told you. I didn't tell you this at first, because I was with you. ⁵But

ᵒ Psalms 35:19, 69:5(4)

now I am going to the One who sent me. "Not one of you is asking me, 'Where are you going?' ⁶Instead, because I have said these things to you, you are overcome with grief. ⁷But I tell you the truth, it is to your advantage that I go away; for if I don't go away, the comforting Counselor will not come to you. However, if I do go, I will send him to you.

⁸"When he comes, he will show that the world is wrong about sin, about righteousness and about judgment — ⁹about sin, in that people don't put their trust in me; ¹⁰about righteousness, in that I am going to the Father and you will no longer see me; ¹¹about judgment, in that the ruler of this world has been judged.

¹²"I still have many things to tell you, but you can't bear them now. ¹³However, when the Spirit of Truth comes, he will guide you into all the truth; for he will not speak on his own initiative but will say only what he hears. He will also announce to you the events of the future. ¹⁴He will glorify me, because he will receive from what is mine and announce it to you. ¹⁵Everything the Father has is mine; this is why I said that he receives from what is mine and will announce it to you.

¹⁶"In a little while, you will see me no more; then, a little while later, you will see me." ¹⁷At this, some of the *talmidim* said to one another, "What is this that he's telling us, 'In a little while, you won't see me; then, a little

Ru·ach Ha·Ko·desh — Holy Spirit
sha·lom — peace
tal·mi·dim — disciples
To·rah — Teaching, "Law"; Pentateuch; Hebrew Bible
Ye·shu·a — Jesus

while later, you will see me"? and, 'I am going to the Father'?" ¹⁸They went on saying, "What is this 'little while'? We don't understand what he's talking about."

¹⁹Yeshua knew that they wanted to ask him, so he said to them, "Are you asking each other what I meant by saying, 'In a little while, you won't see me; and then, a little while later, you will see me'? ²⁰Yes, it's true. I tell you that you will sob and mourn, and the world will rejoice; you will grieve, but your grief will turn to joy. ²¹When a woman is giving birth, she is in pain; because her time has come. But when the baby is born, she forgets her suffering out of joy that a child has come into the world. ²²So you do indeed feel grief now, but I am going to see you again. Then your hearts will be full of joy, and no one will take your joy away from you.

²³"When that day comes, you won't ask anything of me! Yes, indeed! I tell you that whatever you ask from the Father, he will give you in my name. ²⁴Till now you haven't asked for anything in my name. Keep asking, and you will receive, so that your joy may be complete.

²⁵"I have said these these things to you with the help of illustrations; however, a time is coming when I will no longer speak indirectly but will talk about the Father in plain language. ²⁶When that day comes, you will ask in my name. I am not telling you that I will pray to the Father on your behalf, ²⁷for the Father himself loves you, because you have loved me and have believed that I came from God. ²⁸"I came from the Father and have come into the world; again, I am leaving the world and returning to the Father."

²⁹The *talmidim* said to him, "Look, you're talking plainly right now, you're not speaking indirectly at all. ³⁰Now we know that you know everything, and that you don't need to have people put their questions into words. This makes us believe that you came from God."

³¹Yeshua answered, "Now you do believe. ³²But a time is coming — indeed it has come already — when you will be scattered, each one looking out for himself; and you will leave me all alone. Yet I am not alone; because the Father is with me.

³³"I have said these things to you so that, united with me, you may have *shalom*. In the world, you have *tsuris*. But be brave! I have conquered the world!"

17 ¹After Yeshua had said these things, he looked up toward heaven and said, "Father, the time has come. Glorify your Son, so that the Son may glorify you — ²just as you gave him authority over all mankind, so that he might give eternal life to all those whom you have given him. ³And eternal life is this: to know you, the one true God, and him whom you sent, Yeshua the Messiah.

⁴"I glorified you on earth by finishing the work you gave me to do. ⁵Now, Father, glorify me alongside yourself. Give me the same glory I had with you before the world existed.

⁶"I made your name known to the people you gave me out of the world. They were yours, you gave them to me, and they have kept your word. ⁷Now they know that everything you have given me is from you, ⁸because the words you gave me I have given to them, and they have received them. They have really come to know that I came from you, and they have come to trust that you sent me.

⁹"I am praying for them. I am not praying for the world, but for those you have given to me, because they are yours. ¹⁰Indeed, all I have is yours, and all you have is mine, and in them I have been glorified. ¹¹Now I am no longer in the world. They are in the world, but I am coming to you. Holy Father, guard them by the power of your name, which you have given to me, so that they may be one, just as we are. ¹²When I was with them, I guarded them by the power of your name, which you have given to me; yes, I kept watch over them; and not one of them was destroyed (except the one meant for destruction, so that the *Tanakh* might be fulfilled). ¹³But now, I am coming to you; and I say these things while I am still in the world so that they may have my joy made complete in themselves.

¹⁴"I have given them your word, and the world hated them, because they do not belong to the world — just as I myself do not belong to the world. ¹⁵I don't ask you to take them out of the world, but to protect them from the Evil One. ¹⁶They do not belong to the world, just as I do not belong to the world. ¹⁷Set them apart for holiness by means of the truth — your word is truth. ¹⁸Just as you sent me into the world, I have sent them into the world. ¹⁹On their behalf I am setting myself apart for holiness, so that they too may be set apart for holiness by means of the truth.

²⁰"I pray not only for these, but also for those who will trust in me because of their word, ²¹that they may all be one. Just as you, Father, are united with me and I with you, I pray that they may be united with us, so that the world may believe that you sent me. ²²The glory which you have given to me, I have given to them; so

that they may be one, just as we are one — ²³I united with them and you with me, so that they may be completely one, and the world thus realize that you sent me, and that you have loved them just as you have loved me.

²⁴"Father, I want those you have given me to be with me where I am; so that they may see my glory, which you have given me because you loved me before the creation of the world. ²⁵Righteous Father, the world has not known you, but I have known you, and these people have known that you sent me. ²⁶I made your name known to them, and I will continue to make it known; so that the love with which you have loved me may be in them, and I myself may be united with them."

18 ¹After Yeshua had said all this, he went out with his *talmidim* across the stream that flows in winter through the Kidron Valley, to a spot where there was a grove of trees; and he and his *talmidim* went into it. ²Now Y'hudah, who was betraying him, also knew the place; because Yeshua had often met there with his *talmidim*. ³So Y'hudah went there, taking with him a detachment of Roman soldiers and some Temple guards provided by the head *cohanim* and the *P'rushim*; they carried weapons, lanterns and torches. ⁴Yeshua, who knew everything that was going to happen to

---

co·ha·nim — priests
Kid·**ron** — Kedron, Cedron
P'ru·shim — Pharisees
sha·lom — peace
Ta·nakh — Hebrew Scriptures, "Old Testament"
tal·mi·dim — disciples
tsu·ris — troubles
Ye·shu·a — Jesus
Y'hu·dah — Judas

him, went out and asked them, "Whom do you want?" ⁵"Yeshua from Natzeret," they answered. He said to them, "I AM." Also standing with them was Y'hudah, the one who was betraying him. ⁶When he said, "I AM," they went backward from him and fell to the ground. ⁷So he inquired of them once more, "Whom do you want?" and they said, "Yeshua from Natzeret." ⁸"I told you, 'I AM,'" answered Yeshua, "so if I'm the one you want, let these others go." ⁹This happened so that what he had said might be fulfilled, "I have not lost one of those you gave me."

¹⁰Then Shim'on Kefa, who had a sword, drew it and struck the slave of the *cohen hagadol*, cutting off his right ear; the slave's name was Melekh. ¹¹Yeshua said to Kefa, "Put your sword back in its scabbard! This is the cup the Father has given me; am I not to drink it?"

¹²So the detachment of Roman soldiers and their captain, together with the Temple Guard of the Judeans, arrested Yeshua, tied him up, ¹³and took him first to Anan, the father-in-law of Kayafa, who was *cohen gadol* that fateful year. ¹⁴(It was Kayafa who had advised the Judeans that it would be good for one man to die on behalf of the people.) ¹⁵Shim'on Kefa and another *talmid* followed Yeshua. The second *talmid* was known to the *cohen hagadol*, and he went with Yeshua into the courtyard of the *cohen hagadol*; ¹⁶but Kefa stood outside by the gate. So the other *talmid*, the one known to the *cohen hagadol*, went back out and spoke to the woman on duty at the gate, then brought Kefa inside. ¹⁷The woman at the gate said to Kefa, "Aren't you another of that man's *talmidim*?" He said, "No, I'm not."

¹⁸Now the slaves and guards had lit a fire because it was cold, and they were standing around it warming themselves; Kefa joined them and stood warming himself too.

¹⁹The *cohen hagadol* questioned Yeshua about his *talmidim* and about what he taught. ²⁰Yeshua answered, "I have spoken quite openly to everyone; I have always taught in a synagogue or in the Temple where all Jews meet together, and I have said nothing in secret; ²¹so why are you questioning me? Question the ones who heard what I said to them; look, they know what I said." ²²At these words, one of the guards standing by slapped Yeshua in the face and said, "This is how you talk to the *cohen hagadol*?" ²³Yeshua answered him, "If I said something wrong, state publicly what was wrong; but if I was right, why are you hitting me?" ²⁴So Anan sent him, still tied up, to Kayafa the *cohen hagadol*.

²⁵Meanwhile, Shim'on Kefa was standing and warming himself. They said to him, "Aren't you also one of his *talmidim*?" He denied it, saying, "No, I am not." ²⁶One of the slaves of the *cohen hagadol*, a relative of the man whose ear Kefa had cut off, said, "Didn't I see you with him in the grove of trees?" ²⁷So again Kefa denied it, and instantly a rooster crowed.

²⁸They led Yeshua from Kayafa to the governor's headquarters. By now it was early morning. They did not enter the headquarters building because they didn't want to become ritually defiled and thus unable to eat the *Pesach* meal. ²⁹So Pilate went outside to them and said, "What charge are you bringing against this man?" ³⁰They answered, "If he hadn't done something wrong, we wouldn't

have brought him to you." ³¹ Pilate said to them, "You take him and judge him according to your own law." The Judeans replied, "We don't have the legal power to put anyone to death." ³² This was so that what Yeshua had said, about how he was going to die, might be fulfilled.

³³ So Pilate went back into the headquarters, called Yeshua and said to him, "Are you the king of the Jews?" ³⁴ Yeshua answered, "Are you asking this on your own, or have other people told you about me?" ³⁵ Pilate replied, "Am I a Jew? Your own nation and head *cohanim* have handed you over to me; what have you done?" ³⁶ Yeshua answered, "My kingship does not derive its authority from this world's order of things. If it did, my men would have fought to keep me from being arrested by the Judeans. But my kingship does not come from here." ³⁷ "So then," Pilate said to him, "you are a king, after all." Yeshua answered, "You say I am a king. The reason I have been born, the reason I have come into the world, is to bear witness to the truth. Every one who belongs to the truth listens to me." ³⁸ Pilate asked him, "What is truth?"

Having said this, Pilate went outside again to the Judeans and told them, "I don't find any case against him. ³⁹ However, you have a custom that at Passover I set one prisoner free. Do you want me to set free for you the 'king of the Jews'?" ⁴⁰ But they yelled back, "No, not this man but Bar-Abba!" (Bar-Abba was a revolutionary.)

19 ¹ Pilate then took Yeshua and had him flogged. ² The soldiers twisted thorn-branches into a crown and placed it on his head, put a purple robe on him, ³ and went up to him,

saying over and over, "Hail, 'king of the Jews'!" and hitting him in the face.

⁴ Pilate went outside once more and said to the crowd, "Look, I'm bringing him out to you to get you to understand that I find no case against him." ⁵ So Yeshua came out, wearing the thorn-branch crown and the purple robe. Pilate said to them, "Look at the man!" ⁶ When the head *cohanim* and the Temple guards saw him they shouted, "Put him to death on the stake! Put him to death on the stake!" Pilate said to them, "You take him out yourselves and put him to death on the stake, because I don't find any case against him." ⁷ The Judeans answered him, "We have a law; according to that law, he ought to be put to death, because he made himself out to be the Son of God." ⁸ On hearing this, Pilate became even more frightened.

⁹ He went back into the headquarters and asked Yeshua, "Where are you from?" But Yeshua didn't answer. ¹⁰ So Pilate said to him, "You refuse to speak to me? Don't you understand that it is in my power either to set you free or to have you executed on the stake?" ¹¹ Yeshua answered, "You would have no power over me if it hadn't been given to you from above;

A·nan — Annas
Bar-Ab·ba — Barabbas
co·ha·nim — priests
co·hen (ha)·ga·dol — high priest
Ka·ya·fa — Caiaphas
Ke·fa — Peter
Me·lekh — Malchus
Na·tze·ret — Nazareth
Pe·sach — Passover
P'ru·shim — Pharisees
Shim·'on Ke·fa — Simon Peter
tal·mid (pl. *tal·mi·dim*) — disciple
Ye·shu·a — Jesus
Y'hu·dah — Judas

this is why the one who handed me over to you is guilty of a greater sin." [12]On hearing this, Pilate tried to find a way to set him free; but the Judeans shouted, "If you set this man free, it means you're not a 'Friend of the Emperor'! Everyone who claims to be a king is opposing the Emperor!" [13]When Pilate heard what they were saying, he brought Yeshua outside and sat down on the judge's seat in the place called The Pavement (in Aramaic, Gabta); [14]it was about noon on Preparation Day of *Pesach*. He said to the Judeans, "Here's your king!" [15]They shouted, "Take him away! Take him away! Put him to death on the stake!" Pilate said to them, "You want me to execute your king on a stake?" The head *cohanim* answered, "We have no king but the Emperor." [16]Then Pilate handed Yeshua over to them to have him put to death on the stake.

So they took charge of Yeshua. [17]Carrying the stake himself he went out to the place called Skull (in Aramaic, Gulgolta). [18]There they nailed him to the stake along with two others, one on either side, with Yeshua in the middle. [19]Pilate also had a notice written and posted on the stake; it read,

YESHUA FROM NATZERET THE KING OF THE JEWS

[20]Many of the Judeans read this notice, because the place where Yeshua was put on the stake was close to the city; and it had been written in Hebrew, in Latin and in Greek. [21]The Judeans' head *cohanim* therefore said to Pilate, "Don't write, 'The King of the Jews', but 'He said, "I am King of the Jews."'" [22]Pilate answered, "What I have written, I have written."

[23]When the soldiers had nailed Yeshua to the stake, they took his clothes and divided them into four shares, a share for each soldier, with the under-robe left over. Now the under-robe was seamless, woven in one piece from top to bottom; [24]so they said to one another, "We shouldn't tear it in pieces; let's draw for it." This happened in order to fulfill the words from the *Tanakh*,

> "They divided my clothes among themselves
> and gambled for my robe."[p]

This is why the soldiers did these things.
[25]Nearby Yeshua's execution stake stood his mother, his mother's sister Miryam the wife of Klofah, and Miryam from Magdala. [26]When Yeshua saw his mother and the *talmid* whom he loved standing there, he said to his mother, "Mother, this is your son." [27]Then he said to the *talmid*, "This is your mother." And from that time on, the *talmid* took her into his own home.

[28]After this, knowing that all things had accomplished their purpose, Yeshua, in order to fulfill the words of the *Tanakh*, said, "I'm thirsty." [29]A jar full of cheap sour wine was there; so they soaked a sponge in the wine, stuck it on the end of a hyssop branch and held it up to his mouth. [30]After Yeshua had taken the wine, he said, "It is accomplished!" And, letting his head droop, he delivered up his spirit.

[31]It was Preparation Day, and the Judeans did not want the bodies to remain on the stake on *Shabbat*, since it was an especially important *Shabbat*. So they asked Pilate to have the legs broken and the bodies removed. [32]The

---

p Psalm 22:19(18)

31

soldiers came and broke the legs of the first man who had been put on a stake beside Yeshua, then the legs of the other one; ³³ but when they got to Yeshua and saw that he was already dead, they didn't break his legs. ³⁴ However, one of the soldiers stabbed his side with a spear, and at once blood and water flowed out. ³⁵ The man who saw it has testified about it, and his testimony is true. And he knows that he tells the truth, so you too can trust. ³⁶ For these things happened in order to fulfill this passage of the *Tanakh*:

"**Not one of his bones will be broken.**"*q*

³⁷ And again, another passage says,

"**They will look at him whom they have pierced.**"*r*

³⁸ After this, Yosef of Ramatayim, who was a *talmid* of Yeshua, but a secret one out of fear of the Judeans, asked Pilate if he could have Yeshua's body. Pilate gave his consent, so Yosef came and took the body away. ³⁹ Also Nakdimon, who at first had gone to see Yeshua by night, came with some seventy pounds of spices — a mixture of myrrh and aloes. ⁴⁰ They took Yeshua's body and wrapped it up in linen sheets with the spices, in keeping with Judean burial practice. ⁴¹ In the vicinity of where he had been executed was a garden, and in the garden was a new tomb in which no one had ever been buried. ⁴² So, because it was Preparation Day for the Judeans, and because the tomb was close by, that is where they buried Yeshua.

20 ¹ Early on the first day of the week, while it was still dark, Miryam from Magdala went to the tomb and saw that the stone had been removed from the tomb. ² So she came running to Shim'on Kefa and the other *talmid*, the one Yeshua loved, and said to them, "They've taken the Lord out of the tomb, and we don't know where they've put him!"

³ Then Kefa and the other *talmid* started for the tomb. ⁴ They both ran, but the other *talmid* outran Kefa and reached the tomb first. ⁵ Stooping down, he saw the linen burial-sheets lying there but did not go in. ⁶ Then, following him, Shim'on Kefa arrived, entered the tomb and saw the burial-sheets lying there, ⁷ also the cloth that had been around his head, lying not with the sheets but in a separate place and still folded up. ⁸ Then the other *talmid*, who had arrived at the tomb first, also went in; he saw, and he trusted. ⁹ (They had not yet come to understand that the *Tanakh* teaches that the Messiah has to rise from the dead.)

---

co·ha·*nim* — priests
Gab·ta — elevated place(?)
Gul·gol·ta — Golgotha, Calvary
Ke·**fa** — Peter
Klo·**fah** — Clopas
Mir·**yam** — Miriam, Mary
Mir·**yam** from Mag·**da**·la — Mary Magdalene
Nak·di·**mon** — Nicodemus
Na·tze·ret — Nazareth
Pe·sach — Passover
Ra·ma·ta·yim — Arimathea
Shab·**bat** — the Sabbath
Shim·'on Ke·**fa** — Simon Peter
tal·**mid** — disciple
Ta·**nakh** — Hebrew Scriptures, "Old Testament"
Ye·shu·a — Jesus
Yo·sef — Joseph

---

q   Psalm 34:21(20), Exodus 12:46, Numbers 9:12

r   Zechariah 12:10

¹⁰ So the *talmidim* returned home, ¹¹ but Miryam stood outside crying. As she cried, she bent down, peered into the tomb, ¹² and saw two angels in white sitting where the body of Yeshua had been, one at the head and one at the feet. ¹³ "Why are you crying?" they asked her. "They took my Lord," she said to them, "and I don't know where they have put him."

¹⁴ As she said this, she turned around and saw Yeshua standing there, but she didn't know it was he. ¹⁵ Yeshua said to her, "Lady, why are you crying? Whom are you looking for?" Thinking he was the gardener, she said to him, "Sir, if you're the one who carried him away, just tell me where you put him; and I'll go and get him myself." ¹⁶ Yeshua said to her, "Miryam!" Turning, she cried out to him in Hebrew, "*Rabbani!*" (that is, "Teacher!") ¹⁷ "Stop holding onto me," Yeshua said to her, "because I haven't yet gone back to the Father. But go to my brothers, and tell them that I am going back to my Father and your Father, to my God and your God." ¹⁸ Miryam of Magdala went to the *talmidim* with the news that she had seen the Lord and that he had told her this.

¹⁹ In the evening that same day, the first day of the week, when the *talmidim* were gathered together behind locked doors out of fear of the Judeans, Yeshua came, stood in the middle and said, "*Shalom aleikhem!*" ²⁰ Having greeted them, he showed them his hands and his side. The *talmidim* were overjoyed to see the Lord. ²¹ "*Shalom aleikhem!*" Yeshua repeated. "Just as the Father sent me, I myself am also sending you." ²² Having said this, he breathed on them and said to them, "Receive the *Ruach HaKodesh*! ²³ If you forgive someone's sins, their sins are forgiven; if you hold them, they are held."

²⁴ Now T'oma (the name means "twin"), one of the Twelve, was not with them when Yeshua came. ²⁵ When the other *talmidim* told him, "We have seen the Lord," he replied, "Unless I see the nail marks in his hands, put my finger into the place where the nails were and put my hand into his side, I refuse to believe it."

²⁶ A week later his *talmidim* were once more in the room, and this time T'oma was with them. Although the doors were locked, Yeshua came, stood among them and said, "*Shalom aleikhem!*" ²⁷ Then he said to T'oma, "Put your finger here, look at my hands, take your hand and put it into my side. Don't be lacking in trust, but have trust!" ²⁸ T'oma answered him, "My Lord and my God!" ²⁹ Yeshua said to him, "Have you trusted because you have seen me? How blessed are those who do not see, but trust anyway!"

³⁰ In the presence of the *talmidim* Yeshua performed many other miracles which have not been recorded in this book. ³¹ But these which have been recorded are here so that you may trust that Yeshua is the Messiah, the Son of God, and that by this trust you may have life because of who he is.

21 ¹ After this, Yeshua appeared again to the *talmidim* at Lake Tiberias. Here is how it happened: ² Shim'on Kefa and T'oma (his name means "twin") were together with Natan'el from Kanah in the Galil, the sons of Zavdai, and two other *talmidim*. ³ Shim'on Kefa said, "I'm going fishing." They said to him, "We're coming with you." They went and got into the boat, but that night they didn't catch anything. ⁴However, just as day was breaking, Yeshua stood on shore, but the *talmidim* didn't know it was he. ⁵He said to them, "You don't have any fish, do you?" "No," they answered him. ⁶He said to them, "Throw in your net to starboard and you will catch some." So they threw in their net, and there were so many fish in it that they couldn't haul it aboard. ⁷The *talmid* Yeshua loved said to Kefa, "It's the Lord!" On hearing it was the Lord, Shim'on Kefa threw on his coat, because he was stripped for work, and plunged into the lake; ⁸but the other *talmidim* followed in the boat, dragging the net full of fish; for they weren't far from shore, only about a hundred yards. ⁹When they stepped ashore, they saw a fire of burning coals with a fish on it, and some bread. ¹⁰Yeshua said to them, "Bring some of the fish you have just caught." ¹¹Shim'on Kefa went up and dragged the net ashore. It was full of fish, 153 of them; but even with so many, the net wasn't torn. ¹²Yeshua said to them, "Come and have breakfast." None of the *talmidim* dared to ask him, "Who are you?" They knew it was the Lord. ¹³Yeshua came, took the bread and gave it to them, and did the same with the fish. ¹⁴This was now the third time Yeshua had appeared to the *talmidim* after being raised from the dead.

¹⁵After breakfast, Yeshua said to Shim'on Kefa, "Shim'on Bar-Yochanan, do you love me more than these?" He replied, "Yes, Lord, you know I'm your friend." He said to him, "Feed my lambs." ¹⁶A second time he said to him, "Shim'on Bar-Yochanan, do you love me?" He replied, "Yes, Lord, you know I'm your friend." He said to him, "Shepherd my sheep." ¹⁷The third time he said to him, "Shim'on

Bar-Yochanan, are you my friend?" Shim'on was hurt that he questioned him a third time: "Are you my friend?" So he replied, "Lord, you know everything! You know I'm your friend!" Yeshua said to him, "Feed my sheep! ¹⁸Yes, indeed! I tell you, when you were younger, you put on your clothes and went where you wanted. But when you grow old, you will stretch out your hands, and someone else will dress you and carry you where you do not want to go." ¹⁹He said this to indicate the kind of death by which Kefa would bring glory to God. Then Yeshua said to him, "Follow me!"

²⁰Kefa turned and saw the *talmid* Yeshua especially loved following behind, the one who had leaned against him at the supper and had asked, "Who is the one who is betraying you?" ²¹On seeing him, Kefa said to Yeshua, "Lord, what about him?" ²²Yeshua said to him, "If I want him to stay on until I come, what is it to you? You, follow me!" ²³Therefore the word spread among the brothers that

Ga·lil, the — Galilee
Ka·nah — Cana
Ke·fa — Peter
Mir·yam — Miriam, Mary
Mir·yam from Mag·da·la — Mary Magdalene
Na·tan·'el — Nathanael
Na·tze·ret — Nazareth
Rab·ba·ni — my great one, my teacher
Ru·ach-Ha Ko·desh — Holy Spirit
Sha·lom a·lei·khem! — Peace be upon you(pl.)! (greeting)
Shim'on Bar-Yo·cha·nan — Simon, son of John
Shim·'on Ke·fa — Simon Peter
tal·mid (pl. *tal·mi·dim*) — disciple
Ta·nakh — Hebrew Scriptures, "Old Testament"
T·'o·ma — Thomas
Ye·shu·a — Jesus
Zav·dai — Zebedee

that *talmid* would not die. However, Yeshua didn't say he wouldn't die, but simply, "If I want him to stay on until I come, what is it to you?"

²⁴ This one is the *talmid* who is testifying about these things and who has recorded them.

And we know that his testimony is true.

²⁵ But there are also many other things Yeshua did; and if they were all to be recorded, I don't think the whole world could contain the books that would have to be written!

ABOUT THE TRANSLATOR

David H. Stern was born in Los Angeles in 1935, the great-grandson of two of the city's first twenty Jews. He earned a Ph.D. in economics at Princeton University and was a professor at UCLA, mountain-climber, co-author of a book on surfing and owner of health-food stores.

In 1972 he came to faith in Yeshua the Messiah, after which he received a Master of Divinity degree at Fuller Theological Seminary and did graduate work at the University of Judaism.

He was married in 1976 to Martha Frankel, also a Messianic Jew, and together they served one year on the staff of Jews for Jesus. Dr. Stern taught Fuller Theological Seminary's first course in "Judaism and Christianity", organized Messianic Jewish conferences and leaders' meetings, and was an officer of the Messianic Jewish Alliance of America.

In 1979 the Stern family made *aliyah* [immigrated to Israel]. They now live in Jerusalem with their two children and are active in the *Netivyah* congregation and in Israel's Messianic Jewish community.

Dr. Stern is the author of *Messianic Jewish Manifesto*, which outlines the destiny, identity, history, theology and program of today's Messianic Jewish movement, and of *Restoring the Jewishness of the Gospel*, which consists of excerpts from the former book selected for Christians to whom the Jewishness of the Gospel is an unfamiliar idea.

With the publication of the *Jewish New Testament* he is preparing a companion volume, the *Jewish New Testament Commentary*, which will discuss, verse-by-verse, Jewish issues raised in the New Testament — questions Jews have about Yeshua, the New Testament and Christianity; questions Christians have about Judaism and the Jewish roots of their faith; and questions Messianic Jews have about their own identity and role Also, the Complete Jewish Bible is in progress.

These books are available through

JEWISH NEW TESTAMENT PUBLICATIONS
Post Office Box 1313, Clarksville, Maryland 21029, USA